The Word in the World

Prayers for Christian Worship
Book 2

The Word in the World

Compiled by
Donald Hilton

NCEC

Other books by Donald Hilton

Celebrating Series
Risks of Faith
Raw materials of Faith
Results of Faith
After Much Discussion

Compiled by Donald Hilton

Prayers for the Church Community
(with Roy Chapman)
Liturgy of Life
Flowing Streams
Seasons and Celebrations

Cover design by: Peggy Chapman
Illustrations by: Wendy Carolan

Published by:
National Christian Education Council
1020 Bristol Road
Selly Oak
Birmingham
B29 6LB

British Library Cataloguing-in-Publication Data:
A catalogue record for this book is available from the British Library.

ISBN 0 - 7197 - 0900 - 8

First published 1997

Designed and typeset by Kirsteen Rogers, National Christian Education Council
Printed by Ebenezer Baylis & Son Ltd

Contents

	Page
Preface	*vii*
The Church at Worship:	1
Invocation	3
Adoration	8
Confession	16
Thanksgiving	25
Supplication and Intercession	30
Commitment	38
The Lord's Supper	41
Vestry Prayers	57
The Church Community:	65
A local and International Community	67
A Reconciled Community	82
Mission and Ministry:	89
Communicating the Gospel	91
Learning and Teaching	106
Silence and Reflection	118
Justice, peace, and Reconciliation	124
The servant Church	133
The World around us:	141
The Created World	143
The Seasons	150
Conservation and the Care of the Earth	165
Work and Leisure	174
Human Need	183
Christian Life-style:	187
Home and Family	189
Fruits of the Spirit	198
Forgiveness and Reconciliation	204
Following Jesus	209
Personal Service	216
Responding to Suffering	220
Offertory Prayers	227
Closing Prayers and Blessings	233
Prayers before Meetings:	239
Business Meetings	241
Study Groups	243
House Groups	245
Contributors	247
Index of First Lines	249
Index of First Lines by Section	259

The World in the World is a collection of original prayers for occasions when Christians meet for worship. Themes include Mission and Ministry, the World Around Us, and Christian Life-style. Other sections offer prayers to be used before worship, at the offertory, and before study groups or business meetings.

In each section the prayers are arranged in the following liturgical order: Invocation, Adoration, Confession, Thanksgiving, Supplication, Intercession and Commitment. Those parts of the prayers which are printed in bold type can be used as a congregational response. The biblical quotations at the beginning of each section are from the *Revised English Bible.*

The prayers are written by an ecumenical group of writers, most of whom regularly lead worship in local churches, thus giving an immediacy and urgency to the prayers. The variety of styles of the individual writers has been retained to provide a rich collection of prayers, which I hope will be useful in a wide range of local situations.

Like its popular companion volume, *Seasons and Celebrations, The World in the World* is ideal for ministers and local preachers who are regularly responsible for leading worship. It is also helpful for those who lead worship at fellowship meetings, youth meetings and Bible study groups, and as an aid to private devotion.

This collection is offered in the hope that it will enrich the worship of the people of God as they meet to praise the God and Father of our Lord Jesus Christ.

Donald Hilton
Leeds
1997

The Church at Worship

Let all the earth acclaim the Lord!

Worship the Lord in gladness;
enter his presence with joyful songs.

Acknowledge that the Lord is God;
he made us and we are his,
his own people, the flock which he shepherds.
Enter his gates with thanksgiving,
his courts with praise.

Give thanks to him and bless his name;
for the Lord is good and his love is everlasting,
his faithfulness endures to all generations.

Psalm 100

1

This day and all days
are yours, Lord God.
And this day, and all days,
you give reason for us to rejoice and be glad,
for you have loved the world
in Jesus your Son,
once and for all:
for all days, and all places, for all time.
We bring our offering of praise,
in token return for your gift.
In Jesus' name we meet;
in Jesus' name we pray.

2

Heavenly Father,
we willingly draw near to you this day.
Not warily –
  as if you are some fatal disease
But still carefully –
  because you are life-threatening.
To follow you is death itself –
  death to our selfishness,
  death to our pride,
  death to our arrogance.

But still we come,
Because you are the God of resurrection.
Beyond death is new life;
A life we are called to live each day:
Dying to self and living to you.

And this is all in your strength,
For which we pray
In the name of Jesus –
  whose cross is both dead wood
  and living hope.

3

Loving God,
open our eyes to the beauty of your holiness;
open our ears to the message of your word;
open our minds to the challenge of your truth;
open our hearts to the power of your love.
Open our lives to the coming of your Spirit,
that we may truly worship you,
now and forever.

4

Today is a day of celebration – celebration for the Church!
We recall the mighty acts of God:
the Creation of the world,
the bringing into being of all that is and is to be;
the Resurrection of Jesus, the Son of God,
who brought God closer to us, even into the world;
the coming of the Spirit at Pentecost
into the hearts and minds of the disciples
and all who have faith in God.
We celebrate the goodness of God:
focus ourselves on him;
sing his praise, and offer our prayers;
hear his word and seek his guidance.

5

Father, you are closer to us than the air we breathe,
And yet, Almighty God,
you are beyond the range of radio wave, telescope sight or radar search.

Father, your touch is as gentle as a snowflake,
And yet, Almighty God,
yours is the power which spoke the universe into being.

Father, we know you as a loving parent, intimate and close,
And yet, Almighty God,
we can never know you –
our imagination is not lively enough,
our minds too small.

Near us and beyond us,
Father and Almighty God, help us to worship you.

6

Most holy, most lovely God, you have called us from many places and wooed us with many voices. Gently, persistently, you have asked us to take our place among the friends and followers of Jesus, and this we do mostly with joy, though sometimes it is through clenched teeth.

As we offer you our worship this day, hear the silent murmurs of our souls for it is there that our following of Jesus is formed.

Most holy, most lovely God, as we meet together, we join our worship with those of every age who have followed in the Way: with those who have loved amidst hatred; with those who have comforted the afflicted; with those who have suffered in body and mind, and not counted the cost.

Grant to us courage and love, that we may witness to the glory we find in Christ; the glory which offers new paths to the wayward, wisdom to the foolish, a feast to the poor in spirit, and a party to the lonely.

May the light and leaven of your grace work its mystery in us today.

7

Lord of the morning and of all our days and nights, we gather to praise you this new day. We thank you for all your gifts, and praise you for all your care. For you are Maker of all we see and know, Giver of all good gifts, and Lover of us all.
You are Friend in all our lives, reaching out your hand to the stranger, to embrace with strength and hope.
You are Guide for all our days, giving us wisdom, showing us the way to be.
Lord of the morning and of all our days and nights, we gather to praise you this new day, in Jesus' name.

8

This day, as are all days, loving God,
is the day to worship you.
This time, as are all times, loving God,
is the time to give you praise.
This moment, as are all moments, loving God,
is the moment to turn to you in faith.

And so, this day, at this time, from this moment onwards,
  we worship you,
  we praise you,
  we turn again in faith.
Fill our hearts with joy and gladness, we pray,
and take away strain and stress,
that we may feel free to worship you
with our whole beings.
In Christ's name.

9

Almighty and eternal God,
we come before your presence singing.
From all that we are,
for all that you are,
we offer our love to you.

You are our Maker and Minder:
in you, darkness becomes light;
chaos becomes order;
and the desert bears fruit.

You are our Friend:
reaching out a hand of forgiveness and hope
through Jesus to the world;
embracing us with strength and courage.

You are our Guide:
breathing your Spirit in us and between us,
so that we can know your grace in our lives
and show your grace to the world.

Loving God, Maker and Minder, Friend and Guide,
we come before you now in worship,
in Jesus' name.

10

Gracious God,
give us the ears to hear your voice,
the eyes to see your glory,
the hearts to know your love,
and then the will to worship –
    for you are God,
    we are your people,
    and it is right that we offer you praise.
Bless our time together,
and bless us as we go,
that here and at home
we may know your ceaseless presence
in the power of your Spirit.
In the name of our living Lord Jesus Christ.

11

God is love,
and where true love is
God himself is there.

Loving Father, be with us now,
renewing us with your creative love.

Loving Son, be with us now,
bringing forgiveness through your saving love.

Loving Spirit, be with us now,
strengthening us with your sustaining love.

Loving God, Father, Son, and Spirit,
as we worship,
may we be built up in love.

12

Lord our God,
you create and you sustain.
You are with us in the rhythm of work and rest,
    in the pattern of praise and silence,
    in the balance of silent prayer and spoken word,
    and in the spontaneity of friendship and love.
You are with us all our days.
Make us aware of your presence now
as we crown life with worship.
In the name of Jesus
whose renewing life we celebrate this day.

13

Lord our God, King of the universe,
in the beginning you made all things out of nothing,
with no help and no tricks,
but with lots of love.
You were there as the universe grew:
as light exploded
and forces broke free;
as atoms emerged
and stars flamed with brilliance.
Your love made the Earth:
the high mountains and rolling plains;
the churning rivers and deep oceans.
With green and gold and blue,
you brought colour to the world,
shimmering in the sunlight.
You made grass and softness,
trees and shade,
flowers and fragrance.
You made animals:
the giant dinosaur and the itchiest flea;
the scampering hamster
and the water-spouting whale.
And, Lord, in your ingenuity and strength,
you made us in your image:
vulnerable and fragile;
capable of great things
and able to love all that you have made.
Mighty and powerful God, you are a caring Father,
involved in our life and our growing.
We praise you!

14

God of beauty and power, wonder and light,
we worship you for being who you are:
more beautiful than the sunlight you made;
stronger than the power that formed the universe;
brighter than the light which banishes night;
more wonderful than butterfly wings, snowflake's fall, or rising dew.
We worship you in adoration and praise.

15

Lord, we experience you like the sea.
At times we feel you close;
lapping around our lives,
cooling and cleansing.
At other times, you seem far away;
there are spans of sand to cross
before we feel your forgiveness.

When we tread with painful feet,
struggling to find you;
wash our feet,
remove the gritty sand of life:
the mistakes which irritate;
the frustrations that rub away at us;
the sins that wear us down,
making the walk ahead more difficult.
Cleanse us from the past
for service in the future.

Lord, we experience you like the sea.
At times we are afraid of the power of your waves,
and we paddle on the edges of faith,
not wanting to be too deeply committed.
We fear we might be submerged
in the undertow of needs around us,
or lose control if we get out of our depth.

Lord, help us to discover the buoyant freedom
which faith can give.
Help us in this worship to strike out,
supported by your love.
Be with us in the storms of life,
calming our fears,
assuring us of a safe harbour.
Through Jesus Christ our Lord.

16

Creator God,
we praise you for the immensity of your love:
the love that brought the universe to birth;
the love that designed and ordered our world;
the love that breathed life into humankind.
Creator God,
we praise you for the immensity of your love.

Saving God,
we praise you for the endurance of your love:
the love that came to share our human life;
the love that died for us upon the cross;
the love that triumphed over hatred and death.
Saving God,
we praise you for the endurance of your love.

Strengthening God,
we praise you for the power of your love:
the love that brought your Church to life;
the love that transforms hearts and minds;
the love that dares and cares and unites.
Strengthening God,
we praise you for the power of your love.

17

Lord, your love for us brings a smile to our faces
as we share the joy of being alive.
Lord, your love for us brings wonder into our hearts
as we see the beauty of your creation.
Lord, your love for us brings tears into our eyes
as we remember the pain you carry for humanity.
Lord, your love for us makes us shout out loud
as we cannot keep quiet about you.
Lord, your love for us makes us silent
as no words can express our feelings for you.

Silence

18

To be surrounded by a world of beauty and wonder,
to be awakened from refreshing sleep,
to witness the glory of the seasons,
to feel the warmth of the sun, the cooling breeze, the dampness of rain,
is to appreciate and know the love of the creator, our Father God.
God is good: **We praise him.**

To be surrounded by the affection and trust of friends,
to feel the supporting love of the fellowship of the Church,
to hear a reassuring word, to see an encouraging smile,
is to know God's Son Jesus among us
with his healing touch and renewing grace.
God is good: **We praise him.**

To be surrounded by the atmosphere of worship,
to feel a sense of purpose and faith,
to come with a longing to know God more clearly,
to love him more dearly, and follow him more nearly,
is to know the Holy Spirit alive in our midst.
He is here – his power is in us all.
God is good: **We praise him.**

To be surrounded by the majesty, the humanity and the daily strength of Father, Son and Holy Spirit, is to know ourselves richly blessed, deeply forgiven, strongly inspired and wonderfully loved each new morning. For this daily miracle we are moved to say, over and again, 'Yes!'
God is good: **We praise him.**

19

Lord of patterns and rhythms,
you are present in the beauty and order of mathematics,
in the passion and peace of music,
and the form and elegance of art.
We praise you with our minds, our voices and our eyes.

Lord of movement and poise,
you are present in sport and dance,
in children's play and gymnast's balance.
We praise you with our bodies and hearts.

Lord of stillness and vision,
you are present in work and relaxation,
in solitary thought and energetic discussion,
in quiet reflection and eager anticipation.
We praise you with our lives and with our hope.

Lord of our lives, we praise you with all our being.

20

Gracious God,
ever faithful, ever true,
our words of praise are inadequate.
How can we speak of you in your greatness?
Silence alone seems fitting
to reflect the wonder and awe
of your unending presence.

Silence

But we break the silence for we must speak.
We must tell out our love for you.
We must search for words
that somehow declare you are our God:
Father, Son and Spirit;
words that somehow say
we are your people, and we praise you.

Loving God,
in silence and in speaking,
our hearts lift to offer worship,
for you are the light of creation's dawn,
you are the very breath of our lives;
you are the promise of renewal;
you are the offer of forgiveness;
you are the flame of inspiration;
you are the wind of challenging change.

You are our God, we are your people.
We worship you.

21

God of all life, of all ages, of all places;
God of all people, of all voices, of all accents;
God of all signs, of all symbols, of all songs ...

When creation came to be, you held its hand;
when the earth was first flooded with light,
it was you who shielded its eyes.
You are the persisting presence, always, ever alert.

As old or as ancient as you are,
we also know you as the very new within us –
as the soft, the tender, the emerging,
the ever-young, whatever our age.

God of all life, as we worship you this day,
encircle us with the tenderness of your strength;
embrace us with the sweet iron of your mercy,
that within your love we might be touched
by the wisdom of the ages
and be beckoned by the spirit of tomorrow.

Within your enfolding we know you as the life-giver,
the befriender, the travelling companion,
the fleeting memory, the lover and the hunter of us all.

In you we place our trust and open our secret places;
In you we dare the openness to worship;
In you, past and future join hands in adoration.

22

Eternal God of wonder, might and power,
how can we offer humble adoration?
If we bow our heads, our hearts might still be raised in arrogance.
If we kneel, our minds might still stand tall with pride.
If we are silent, inner thoughts might overreach themselves.
If we speak the lowly word, intention might demean our spoken word.
Love us, Lord,
and let your love flood through us, heart and mind, and all.
Then we will love,
and in our loving learn to be with you – and thus adore.

23

Use two voices, one for the Bible readings, the other for the prayer.

Where were you when I laid the earth's foundations? Tell me, if you know and understand. Who set its corner-stone in place, while the morning stars sang in chorus and the sons of God all shouted for joy?

Job 38. 4, 6b-7

How dare we speak your name, creator God,
puny mortals as we are, nothings in a universe of splendour?
Before the earth took form, you were,
and when the earth crumbles, humankind forgotten,
you still will be, forming new worlds, fresh universes.
  And yet, though transient visitors on a fragile globe,
  we join the chorus of the sons of God, and whisper praise and joy.

You it was who fashioned my inward parts; you knitted me together in my mother's womb. I praise you, for you fill me with awe; wonderful you are, and wonderful your works. You know me through and through ...

Psalm 139. 14-15

How dare we lift our eyes to see your face, designer God?
You made our eyes and ears and brain, sinews, muscles, veins and heart.
The potter rules the pot, the painter signs the picture as his own,
and creatures have no claim upon their Maker.
  And yet, though with no rights,
  we take our place with adoration and delight
  amongst the wonders of your fashioned world.

Who knows the mind of the Lord? Who has been his counsellor? From him and through him and for him all things exist – to him be glory for ever.

Romans 11.34, 36

How dare we say we know you, wondrous God?
We paddle in the shallows of your mighty sea;
stumble amongst the foothills of your soaring heights.
Your glory blazes bright, and we exist only because you are.
  And yet, it is enough
  to know that you are God,
  and bend the knee, bow down the heart and worship you alone.

'Praise and honour, glory and might, to him who sits on the throne and to the Lamb for ever!'

Revelation 5.13b

How dare we claim your name, Lamb on the throne?
By nails and thorns, by fractured limbs and broken spirit
you reign supreme: victor and victim, God's own Son.

And yet, you take us by the hand
and hold us in your love,
for you are one with us, and we with you,
and we adore, in wonder, love and praise.

24

Praise to you, Lord our God – King of creation;
Maker and minder of all we know: the very heart of all being.
We praise you.
Your glory is seen in majestic grandeur,
in intricate miniature,
in beauty and truth,
in love, in laughter,
in tears, in joy.

Praise to you, Lord our God – come amongst us.
Redeemer of the world: healing brokenness,
speaking truth,
showing love,
giving self on the Cross in Christ.

Praise to you, Lord our God,
coming now,
giving life,
breathing hope,
lighting minds,
lifting hearts,
falling fresh on all who call.

Praise to you, Lord our God.

25

Praise be to you, our God,
maker of heaven and earth,
the very breath of life within us.
    Praise be to you, our God,
    redeemer of the world,
    the very hope within us.
Praise be to you, our God,
giver of life,
flame of inspiration lighting our way,
guiding our lives.

Praise be to you, our one God,
Father, Son and Spirit.

26

For the joy of a fresh sunrise,
for the hope each new day brings,
for a love that knows no bounds,
we praise you,
bountiful God.

But even as words of praise
pass our lips,
we know that we have not always lived
as those who are loved, forgiven and set free.

We have allowed ourselves
to be imprisoned by tradition,
captivated by habit,
limited by fear.

Through the healing power
of love made flesh,
make us whole,
to live and love
with open hearts
and generous spirits.

27

Compassionate God, we know we are sinners. We look to you for the forgiveness which will release and renew our living.

Forgive us that in our insecurity we often overstep the mark and claim you as our own, and fail to hear you calling all the peoples of the world your Beloved.

Forgive us that in our need for identity we overreach ourselves, and reject those customs and traditions which are not our own.

Forgive us that in our need for affirmation we put others down, and fail to see you kneeling, and lifting all people to the one true God.

Out of the modesty of your love forgive the arrogance we both clearly display and cunningly conceal.

28

Living Jesus, we praise you because you show us that God is love:
love which reaches to *all* people;
love which does not count the cost of loving;
love which never ends.
Forgive us when we love ourselves and not you.

We praise you because you are the *Way*:
you are the way to God;
you lived the way we want to live;
you guide us on God's way of life.
Forgive us when we take our own way and not yours.

We praise you because you are the *Truth*:
you are the truth about God;
you show us the truth about ourselves;
you show us how to live as true human beings.
Forgive us when we think we know better than your truth.

We praise you because you are the *Life*:
you lived life perfectly, without sin;
you give us the example for life;
you help us to live our life to the full.
Forgive us when we live for ourselves and not for you.

Fill us with your Spirit who shows us the way, reveals the truth, and gives us life.

29

Merciful God, we confess that we find it difficult to live Christian lives. We are full of good intentions but are easily swayed from doing and saying what we know we should. We are distracted by busyness and self-interest, and handicapped by lack of confidence, and insensitivity to others. We feel wretched before you, loving Parent. Our sin makes us feel worthless.

Help us to turn our minds away from ourselves and our inadequacies and to focus on you and your forgiving and accepting love, for only you have the power to make us holy. And you, almighty God, will do it.

Thanks be to God.

30

Father, Son and Spirit,
you are One, and we are one in you.
Forgive us, for we rarely achieve such unity.
We belong to a world divided by power and want.
We belong to communities fragmented by fear and superficial politeness.
And we ourselves are broken and incomplete, not achieving what we want,
and doing the wrong we try to avoid.
We are sorry and pray for forgiveness.

Listen, everyone, and hear the good news:
to all who receive him, Jesus gives the power to become the children of God,
and from his fullness, we shall receive grace upon grace.
Thanks be to God.

31

Gracious God, with sorrow we admit
how well we know that our lives
have not been wholly as you will.
We confess the sin we know,
and regret the shame we feel.

We confess that some thoughts have been unworthy:
  centred on self, others denied.
We confess that some words have been wounding:
  barbed and harsh, twisting deep.
We confess that some actions have been unfitting:
  kingdom-destroying, love-denying.
We confess that sometimes we have been silent and still in the face of need:
  hesitant to give, slow to care.

'Remember, Lord, your tender care
  and love unfailing,
for they are from of old.
Do not remember the sins and
  offences of my youth,
but remember me in your unfailing love,
in accordance with your goodness, Lord.'

Psalm 25.6-7

In Christ's name we pray.

32

Lord, so often we exploit what you have made.
We misuse the precious gifts you give us, spoiling the world around us.
We pollute rivers and seas.
We kill animals unnecessarily.
We use other people's weakness to get what we want.
We say things we wish we hadn't, and we fail to speak out when we should.
We are sorry; we are like lost people, not knowing which way to turn.

Listen, everyone, and hear the good news:
God comes to find the lost and take them home.
God rejoices when anyone is truly sorry.
He restores us so that, with people down the ages,
and with everyone in heaven, we can sing,
'Holy, holy, holy Lord God of power and might,
Heaven and Earth are full of your glory,
Hosanna in the highest!'

33

God of our whole lives:
all we have been,
all we are,
all we yet will be;
we confess the sin within us.
Our words and thoughts and deeds
have too often brought misery;
our silent inaction
has too often denied joy.

In Christ you came for outcasts and for sinners.
With sorrow we confess that we create outcasts by our lack of love.
With shame we acknowledge our need of forgiveness.
Our past weighs heavily;
our present holds us captive;
our future seems unclear.
Forgive us, merciful God.
Free us from sin's tyranny,
that our whole lives
might be lived for your glory.

34

God of grace,
forgive our self-concern,
forgive our lack of love,
forgive our ill-judged thoughts.

God of mercy,
forgive our impatience,
forgive our hard hearts,
forgive our harsh words.

God of peace,
forgive our wasting conflict,
forgive our wounding pride,
forgive our careless deeds.
In Jesus' name.

35

Merciful God, forgive our foolish ways.
Forgive our deliberate and wilful sin;
our conscious transgressing
of your perfect will for us.
Forgive, too, the insidious sin
of which we are barely aware,
so conditioned have we become
to its presence in our lives.

Merciful God,
forgive us,
and cleanse us
from all kinds of unrighteousness,
that we might stand
renewed and restored,
freed from the crippling effects
of guilt and despair.
In Christ's name.

36

God of community,
As you lead us through the crowded streets of living,
Where we must learn and change and grow,
We thank you for those who surround us,
Whom we can call sister and brother in Christ.
Thank you for the jumbled family of faith
That we know as your Church.

It is the Church of forgiven sinners;
Of those with bruised knees and wounded hearts
Who have been soothed and salved
By the ointment of your love.

For this diverse and gathered Church we pray:
We pray that we may limp
– so that we will always lean on you.
We pray that we may be weak
– so that we will always need your guidance.
We pray that we may doubt ourselves
– so that we will always trust in you.

In the midst of our living,
We pray that you will guide our steps
So that we walk together;
Refusing to march on ahead,
But humbly waiting for those who lag behind;
Listening, lending an arm and a shoulder,
And willing to become the caring, sharing people
You want your Church to be.

37

Lord of life, we know that you watch over us in loving care;
as does a mother to her newborn babe, a father to his children,
as friend with friend, so intimate and close is your loving;
Yet we confess that in our folly we blindly live
as though we were fatherless orphans,
bereft of mother-love
and lost in friendless solitude.
Enclose us in your care.
Wrap your love around us,
and restore us to our rightful mind.

38 Shining, surprising, grace-full God,
for avoiding the searchlight of your desire for us,
and running away from your love:
Forgive us.

For preferring the safe, familiar and certain,
to the risky, unknown and mysterious:
Forgive us.

For failing to believe in the vulnerability of power,
and the power of vulnerability:
Forgive us.

For taking no delight in variety,
and insisting on sameness and conformity:
Forgive us.

For fearing those different from ourselves,
and projecting onto them what we cannot accept within ourselves:
Forgive us.

For assuming that we are superior to the rest of creation,
for abusing, despoiling, and failing to celebrate our relationship with the earth and the web of life:
Forgive us.

For not noticing your presence in darkness as in light,
in body as in spirit, in feeling as in intellect,
in pain as in healing, in Good Friday as in Easter Day:
Forgive us.

Set us free, we pray, to be whole human beings
and to live our lives graciously and without fear.

Silence

God forgives us:
God makes peace within us:
we claim this healing, in faith and hope.

39

Merciful God,
we confess to you all in our lives that grieves you.

Forgive us for fearing to trust you.
Forgive us for fleeing to gods of our own making,
  as if to find there the succour only you can provide.

Forgive us for wounding with words
  instead of healing with hands.
Forgive us for being quick to anger
  and devoid of steadfast love.
Forgive us for being slow to care
  and abounding in indifference.

Forgive us for forgetting to affirm
  and being too ready to condemn.
Forgive us for treating as duty what should be delight,
  as burden what should be privilege,
  and as intrusion what should be loving sacrifice.

Forgive us for insisting in our own fallenness
  and failing to see your grace at work in our lives.
Forgive us for being too concerned with sin,
  and too little aware of forgiveness.

Lord, in your mercy,
hear our prayer,
and in your mercy, forgive.

40

God, the world is puffed up with over-weening pride.
And we share it.
God, how we share it!
We scorn the vulnerable,
boast of our cleverness,
use knowledge as a way to hang on to power,
show how clever we are by belittling others,
and destroy other people by sharp-edged gossip.
Cleanse and renew your world, God.
Restore it to true humility.
And, as needs must be, begin with us.

41

Word of God, flowing free,
flow in and through us,
to cleanse and bring
a new beginning,
a fresh start,
right relationships
and peace.

When the tide recedes,
leaving a fresh page of sand,
then the time is right for forgiveness.

When the tide is balanced on the horizon,
flowing in on one shore and out on another,
then the time is right for dialogue.

When the tide comes flooding in,
washing clean the beach,
then the time is right to begin again.

Silence

Word of God, flowing free,
flow in and through us,
to cleanse and bring
a new beginning,
a fresh start,
right relationships
and peace.

42

Father and God, who else have we to thank but you:
 for the wonderful world around us
 and the gift of life within us?
Lord Jesus Christ, who else have we to thank but you:
 for the life of the Church through long generations
 and our own fellowship within this place?
Holy Spirit, who else have we to thank but you:
 for the power of goodness sweeping through the ages
 and the urge to wholeness in our own lives?
Father, Son and Holy Spirit, who else have we to thank?
Thank you. Thank you. Thank you.

43

God of love,
we thank you.
In you – is utter strength,
in you – is ultimate goodness,
in you – is complete faithfulness,
in you – is total compassion.

God of love,
we thank you.
From you – the light of your word,
from you – the call to a people,
from you – the promise of grace,
from you – the prospect of life.

God of love,
we thank you.
With us – in your Word become flesh,
with us – in your Son, Jesus Christ,
with us – in your gift for the world,
with us – in your pledge for our peace.

God of love,
we thank you.
For us – in the presence of your Spirit,
for us – in the finding of faith,
for us – in the offer of forgiveness,
for us – in the hope of a new dawn.

God of love, we thank you.

44

Loving and gracious God,
we thank you for your many gifts to us:
for the world which you have made
to provide us with all that we need for life,
and to be our place of pilgrimage;
for the gift of one another,
the caring and sharing, the laughter and tears,
the demands and rewards of loving;
for life itself, with its opportunities,
its challenges, its moments of joy.
For all this, we thank you, Parent God.

We thank you most, faithful God,
for the gift of yourself:
your steadfast and forgiving love for your people
despite their straying hearts
and their acts of disobedience;
and for sending your only Son
to share our human life with us,
to call us back to you,
to die for us upon the cross,
and to be raised again, that we might know
true and eternal life in you.

Loving and gracious God,
we thank you for your many gifts to us.

45

In gladness and thanksgiving we recognize the world as your home and your delight. Help us as Christian women and men to make the earth and its peoples glad, that we may bring new singing to birth in your heart.

In gladness and thankfulness we recognize that the whole of our life is bound up in the mystery of faith, and the life of the Spirit. Our thankfulness reaches out to you in the confidence that you will continue to lead us, nudge us, cajole us, and warn us. Help us as Christian women and men to be living witnesses to the life of the Spirit, within and among the life and desires of the flesh.

Awaken our gratitude again to the wonder and enduring fullness of your passion and mercy. May the earthy, all-embracing nature of your good purposes flood over us, and incorporate our life of faith in that new world you are bringing into being.

46

Lord, we thank you for your love towards us, which continues to reach out to us, even when we turn away.
For the love which called Abraham out in faith, which supported Isaac, and watched Jacob grow and prosper.
For the love which brought the Israelites out of the land of slavery, and found them a land flowing with milk and honey.
For the love which spoke through the prophets, love shown in words of judgement, to bring people back to you.
We thank you for the self-giving love that you showed in giving your Son to be one of us; for the persistence of his love which endured the cross to celebrate the new life of your love released in the Spirit.
We thank you for the love which lives in us, helping us to be patient and kind.
We thank you for the love of family, which supports us and helps us to grow.
We thank you for the love of lovers, which walks on air.
We thank you for the love of Christian fellowship which encourages us, and stretches our hope and endurance to reach towards your Kingdom.

47

Give thanks to God because he is God:
Creator and Parent, Protector and King;
  for every sign of his eternal rule,
  for every opportunity of worship and praise;
  and especially for our being together this day.

Give thanks to God because he has shown himself in Jesus, the Christ:
Saviour and Friend, Lover and Lord;
  for every sign that he is active in the lives of men and women, girls and boys;
  for every opportunity of service;
  and especially for everything in our worship today that calls us to discipleship.

Give thanks to God for the gift of the Holy Spirit:
Comforter and Guide, Inspirer and Encourager;
  for every sign that his love is sweeping through human lives;
  for every opportunity for love to overcome hate, and war to turn to peace;
  and especially for the signs of his presence with us today.

Mighty Creator, challenging Lord, ever-leading Presence,
We give you thanks this day and every day.

48

Lord of rest and relaxation,
on the seventh day you created rest, your work complete.
Coming into your presence, we pause,
seeking rest and relaxation from the rush of days.
But our minds still race:
  there are things we have to remember,
  decisions we have to make,
  tasks we have to do.
Lord, as in the beginning you brought order to chaos,
calm the flow of our thoughts
and help us to worship you.

Silence

Now, Lord of imagination,
in the silence we give you thanks
for all the wonderful ways our minds and bodies work,
and for our dreams and visions,
  for games that stretch us, and prayers that make us reach out,
  for leisure that relaxes us, and glimpses of new exciting work,
  for hopes of a future without tears, and a life without violence,
  for the vision of a world that honours you, and our part in creating it.
Lord, inspire us, so that our visions move us towards you
and we truly worship you.

49

Lord of reality,
we dare to be honest before you.
We come to this day of worship battered by life,
and not sure which way to turn.
Confusion rules the world
and we have contributed to it.

Confession is on our lips
but so is thanksgiving.
We give you thanks for the support of friends and family,
for the conviction that you are with us, day by day,
even when we cannot recognize your presence;
for the deep hope that undergirds all human life,
and for your constancy, steadying the swirls of change and indecision.
Lord, help us to help each other to worship you.

50

Living God,
we are struck by awe
when we think about you –
all that you are for us, all that you have done, and yet do.
We speak, but our words are wholly inadequate,
so profound is their failure to do justice
to your glory and grandeur.
Silence seems our only option;
a silence bathed in an appreciation
of the deep mysteries of faith;
a silence within which your Spirit prays with us,
giving divine expression to our love and our longings.

So, in the silence, hear our thanksgiving.

Silence

In Jesus' name.

51

Life-giving God,
we thank you for your Word made flesh
in Jesus Christ, the true vine.

Thank you that you call us
to be branches joined to the vine,
drinking the good news of your loving guidance
like sap rising from the roots.
Thank you for promising us
fulfilment and fruit-bearing,
purpose, point and direction to all our living.
Thank you for the rich vineyard of your Church.
We pray that the fruits we bear
are not wild, but bountiful,
and pleasing to you.

52 If ever, Lord, we meet to praise your name,
sanctuary-safe within the hallowed walls,
and try by prayer, or hymn, by solemn silence or full-throated praise,
to close the doors and keep the world at bay,
to shade the windows lest the light distracts,
ignore the sounds of traffic, passing feet, bird-song or voice,
then, Lord, rebuke us,
and afresh remind us of your loving care for all that you have made:
its nature: cruel and kind; its people: sinners and saints;
and of a cross, up-reared to save them all.
Then call us back, to worship you aright, in spirit and in truth.

53 Lord, we pray 'give us this day our daily bread!'
We remember before you:
the many in our world for whom daily bread means daily struggle,
and far too often a vain struggle;
our brothers and sisters who are stricken by famine and shortages,
and oversupplied with despair.
Guide and inspire us to share the bounty of the fruitful earth
so that compassion becomes the key, and life the hope.

Lord, we pray 'forgive us our trespasses!'
We remember before you:
the many in our world beset by a sense of paralysing guilt;
those driven by forces within themselves
over which they have little control;
those nursing ancient sins long forgiven by those they once hurt,
and by you.
Release and uplift them
so that they know the offer of freedom and life renewed
that lies at the heart of the gospel.

Lord, we pray 'deliver us from evil!'
We remember before you:
the many in our world beset by evils
of unjust, withering and wasteful conflict,
of oppression from compassionless leaders,
of rejection by the prejudices of communities and wider society.
Redeem and revive your fallen world
so that outcasts know themselves included in the feast of heaven,
and peace and right-purpose is pursued by leaders and trend-setters.
In Jesus' name.

54

Loving God, we come to pray for the world where there is a lack of love.
Your love is patient and kind.
We pray for those looking after relations at home,
and for carers in homes, hospitals and hospices.
May they be supported by love.

Your love is never arrogant, nor boastful, nor rude.
We pray for those who are bullied,
and for those who torment them.
May both find a love that is firm but free.

Your love never insists on getting its own way.
We pray for those in marriages that are stretched to breaking point,
and for those wrapped up in their own selfishness.
We pray for those who are irritable because they are tired.
We pray for those who are resentful because they feel hard done by.
May they know the love which softens hard hearts,
sees both sides of a question,
and is willing to compromise.

Your love never rejoices in the wrong, but only in truth.
We pray for those caught up in corruption or a web of lies,
and for those who feel manipulated or abused.
May they know the love which has integrity and delights in the truth.

Love bears all things,
    and we pray for those who carry burdens beyond their strength.
Love believes all things,
    and we pray for those who struggle with faith,
    and doubt.
Love hopes all things,
    and we pray for those at the end of their tether.
Love endures all things,
    and we pray for those who suffer in silence,
    and those who hunger and thirst for your way of love to prevail.
We ask these prayers in the name of Jesus, your love with a human face.

55

Father God, in the beginning you separated light from dark,
 and land from sea.
In the sea of life we come to worship,
finding an island in time.
In the sea of faith we come to find you,
a lighthouse and a haven.
When the sea is blue,
and we are cruising, calm and controlled,
remind us of your presence, Lord.
Help us to plumb your depths,
that we might know
that the wider the ocean of love,
the deeper is the sense of peace.
 We pray for those who are sailing into life:
 for children, and those who care for them and teach them;
 for those embarking on a new adventure;
 for those celebrating a glad arrival.

When seas are grey and foreboding,
come to us as Christ the pilot,
pointing us to the harbour light.
 We pray for our world:
 for politicians, steering a way through the complexities of life;
 for prophets seeking to read the signs of the times;
 for those around us who feel trapped by circumstances
 or who have lost their way.
Help us to navigate your world,
that we might know
that the larger the island of knowledge,
the longer is the shoreline of wonder.

Lord, when seas are white-capped and overwhelming,
may the Spirit be our rudder and strength.
Calm the tempest, strengthen our faith.
 We pray for those daily buffeted by events:
 those in crisis;
 those who are coping with illness or pain;
 those who grieve.
When our boat is fragile, may your grace hold us together.

56

Lord Jesus, you set a child in our midst as a potent symbol.
Help us to make our prayers honest and innocent of guile, inquisitive and willing.

Lord Jesus, you sweated over a carpenter's bench.
We pray for those in work-places which are understaffed,
and those worried by redundancy.
Strengthen them in their work,
and help them to see life beyond the factory, office or shop.
We pray for those who cannot find work.
Give them renewed dignity
which builds up confidence and a sense of self-worth.

Lord Jesus, you had nowhere to rest your head.
We pray for the homeless, for those on the edge of society
and for those having problems with mortgage repayments and debt.
Help them to find creative ways forward, and guide those who support them.

Lord Jesus, you took Peter's mother-in-law by the hand.
You were touched by a woman seeking healing.
We pray for those who are ill,
for those who know that they will never get better, and for all who care for them.
Quietly we name those known to us ...

Lord Jesus, you wept at the grave of a friend.
We share the tears of those who grieve in bereavement,
for those from whom a loved one has been wrenched by sudden death,
and for those who struggle in loneliness after years of companionship.
We pray for all who mourn, that they will be comforted.

Lord Jesus, you shed tears over Jerusalem.
We pray for our world:
for cities of conflict where politics and race divide;
for nations where peace is fragile amidst the posturing of self-seeking leaders;
for regions of the world where hunger for power clashes with national pride.
We pray longingly for peace with justice to fill our world.

Lord Jesus, you laughed with joy and delight with your friends.
We rejoice with those who celebrate joyous events;
share the delight of families united;
revel in the anticipation of those preparing for marriage,
planning anniversaries, or waiting for the birth of a baby,
and we unite in hope with all who struggle for a brighter future.

57

Loving God, your Kingdom is a kingdom of justice and mercy. We pray for the leaders of the nations, that they might rule fairly and with compassion, respecting the rights and needs of all people and promoting peace.
Today we pray especially for ...
Your Kingdom come. **Your will be done.**

Loving God, your Kingdom is a kingdom of hope and joy. We pray for those in sorrow or need. We remember the bereaved, the anxious and the ill, the destitute, the hungry and the homeless.
Today we pray especially for ...
Your Kingdom come. **Your will be done.**

Loving God, your Kingdom is a kingdom of love and unity. We pray for the church here in ... and the Church throughout the world, asking that we might be true agents of, and witnesses to, your saving love.
Today we pray especially for ...
Your Kingdom come. **Your will be done.**

Loving God, your Kingdom is a kingdom of light and life. We pray for ourselves, that you will guide us safely on our journey through life so that we might come to be with you in your eternal kingdom.
Your Kingdom come. **Your will be done.**

58

Almighty God, the nations rise and fall. In the changes in the fortunes of nations, communities and groups we see our own experience writ large. With sadness we acknowledge that the story of much of our history is of victory going to the strong, and suffering falling on the innocent and the weak.
Merciful God: **Hear us in our prayer this day.**

Give us faith, that in times of difficulty we may be saved from pessimism and despair, that the tears we shed over our history may be more for others than for ourselves. Give us a generous, all-embracing faith that welcomes the world to our hearts, so that our discipleship may add to the salvation of the world and ourselves.
Merciful God: **Hear us in our prayer this day.**

We pray for the broken-hearted, the shocked, the stunned and the beaten, that our tears and our faith may flow for those who are beyond weeping or believing. Sadly we have learned, Lord Jesus, that loving enemies is too much for us on our own. Surround us with wise and saintly friends who will encourage us.
Merciful God: **Hear us in our prayer this day.**

We remember how Jesus prayed for the city and the people who would destroy him. We pray for grace, that we may surprise ourselves in acts of love towards our enemies. We pray for the embittered, the resentful, the hateful, the fearful, and those who hold so fast to pain that they cannot welcome forgiveness, hope or love.
Merciful God: **Hear us in our prayer this day.**

Teach us, O Lord, to mingle our tears with your tears, that the trials and distress which accompany our living may become one with the divine passion which alone will save humankind. It is you alone who will wipe the tears from every eye. It is to you, in the name of Jesus your Son, that we pray.

59

The storms rage,
the waves roll high,
the seas crash.
Lord God, the power of weather is awesome.
The death and destruction it can bring is tragic.

Our stormy world is so full of possible pain.
And so we build defences:
we keep the sea at bay;
we keep the stormy winds out;
we seal ourselves from the rain.

We remember those caught in winds of discontent,
and in storms of pain-bearing passion.
We remember those buffeted by the shock of bad news,
by debilitating illness,
harrowing grief,
disarming doubt.
May they find clement days of strong faith to uphold them,
stilling the storms of their lives.

And when we find ourselves walking sunlit paths,
Guard us – from guarding ourselves too closely.
Keep us – from keeping ourselves away from those in need.
Save us – from saving ourselves the grief of sharing their pain,
and stop us from sealing ourselves from their sorrow;
for in Christ you came to bear human grief,
and call us to share the task with you.

60 Living God,
we pray for the Church and for the world.

Bless your Church here and around the world.
Give your Church a renewed hunger to be about your will;
  a strengthened courage in a world that is often hostile;
  a deepened sense of commitment;
  and the wit and the wisdom to imitate your Son, Jesus Christ, our Lord.

Bless your world and all its nations and peoples.
Deliver it and all its peoples
  from the destruction of violence, and the poison of bitter anger;
  from the web of twisted and perverse hatred;
  from glorying in the pain and loss of others;
  from misplaced pride and a delight in division;
  from all strategy where love is a casualty and enmity is enthroned.
We pray for the victims of violence:
  for lives shattered by intimidation, or terrified by nightmare;
  for families scarred by oppression,
    or ruined by a bruising lack of consideration.

And we pray for ourselves.
Bless us, living God,
with such an overflowing of your love
that we become as bursting dykes of grace flooding the land.

All these things we pray
in the name and for the sake of Jesus Christ
who gives us the way to be, and the way to do,
so that we become your people and do your will.

61 God eternal, all-knowing, and total love,
you see the whole of human life.
You feel its joy and pain.
There is nothing we can tell you about facts or feelings.

We do not come to you with information about which you are ignorant,
nor with a list of what we want you to do.
We come to talk about things which trouble us:
  in your world, in your Church, and in ourselves.

We don't like what is happening in our own society or in the rest of the world ... *Give current examples.*
We feel helpless before such sadness and pain.
Help us to see how our concern can be channelled into positive action.

We are anxious about the Church.
We find it hard to live with its disobedience and are ashamed that we contribute to it ... *Give current examples.*
We suspect that our priorities are wrong
  and that we misunderstand what is true success or failure.
We have no power within ourselves to change.
Help us to create a life together which will demonstrate your love.

We are worried about our friends.
In the silence we think about them and their particular needs.
Silence
Help us to show your love through our love for them,
and thus ourselves become the answer to our prayers,
through Jesus Christ our Lord.

62

Lord of all human life,
even as we meet for worship, the world goes on,
and people live their lives in sadness:
  little children are robbed of their innocence;
  mothers clutch fitful babies to long-dry breasts;
  people walk in fear on city streets;
  the newly unemployed join the tragic queue;
  and gunfire rakes the tattered remains of once-loved homes.

Lord of all human life,
even as we meet for worship, the world goes on,
and people live their lives in joy:
  children laugh, and play, and learn;
  families are held in loving security;
  communities are built on justice, love and care;
  students learn, people train, jobs are found;
  and bridges are built across the war-torn lands.

Lord, as we meet for worship,
give us a renewed solidarity with all your people;
as we weep their tears and share their joy,
renew our hope.
And theirs.

63

Love of the Father,
reaching out in creation;
may we reach out to others.

Love of the Son,
in obedience and self-giving;
may we follow your way.

Love of the Spirit,
active within us;
may we be active in the world.

64

Lord, we have remembered your redeeming love.
May we keep to your way:
bearing each other's burdens;
loving each other as you have loved us;
that the world may know that we are your disciples.
In the name of Jesus, our Lord and Saviour.

65

Loving God,
you have chosen us;
called us to be your children
and agents of your love in the world.

Loving God,
we choose you
to be the centre of our lives.
We choose the way of love.
We choose the way of life.
We choose the way of Christ our Saviour.

Loving God,
you have chosen us,
and we are your people;
we have chosen you,
and you are our eternal Lord.

66

Eternal God, you hold in love all who know and praise you,
    and those who do not.
Lord Jesus Christ, you are a friend to all who own your name,
    and those who ignore you.
Holy Spirit of God, you work in full view of our wondering eyes,
    and where we are blind to your action.
We, who know your love, your friendship and your work,
commit ourselves afresh,
    to declare your love, proclaim your friendship, and reveal your work
    to the people we meet,
so that the day may come when everyone in every place
shouts your name and acclaims your work, with joy and delight.

67

God of all circumstances and places,
when joy has gone from life,
when love has faded,
when peace is lost in the clouds of war,
    still we will work for your Kingdom.
This we promise.

When lies have been enthroned as truth,
when unbelief has been crowned as faith,
when dishonour has received a garland of acclaim,
    still we will work for your Kingdom.
This we promise.

When compassion is called weakness,
when gentleness is disdained,
when kindness is spurned as feeble,
    still we will work for your Kingdom.
This we promise.

When your good name is treated in vain,
when Jesus is crucified again,
when the Spirit is denied,
    still we will work for your Kingdom.
This we promise.

All this we promise,
and from full and thankful hearts,
but only dare to promise
in the confidence that you are by our side.

68 May the God who is perfectly at home amid unloveliness, dirt, disease and disorder, charm us with the simplicity of how the world might be.

May the God whose life is among the poorest, dispel our unfounded fears, that we may see more clearly the true enemies of justice and compassion.

May the Christ, the godliness among us, confirm and quicken our passion for justice; undermine our tactics of resistance; and tantalize us with fresh images of a world renewed.

May the troubling, restless Spirit, who is alive in all creation, gift us with an aperitif of the future, and open us to the good news which comes to the world out of the lives of the poor.

69 Passionate God,
our hearts are stirred to life,
so that our whole being feels like dancing
and singing,
for you are our God,
we are your people.

Passionate God,
intimately involved with the world,
in Jesus Christ your Son,
our Saviour:
grace-giver, joy-completer, life-fulfiller,
we would follow faithfully.

Passionate God,
firing us still with the flames of your Spirit,
we commit ourselves with passion
to the cause of your Kingdom,
for the love of Christ,
in whose name we pray.

The Lord's Supper

For the tradition which I handed on to you came to me from the Lord himself: that on the night of his arrest the Lord Jesus took bread, and after giving thanks to God broke it and said: 'This is my body, which is for you; do this in memory of me.' In the same way, he took the cup after supper, and said: 'This cup is the new covenant sealed by my blood. Whenever you drink it, do this in memory of me.' For every time you eat this bread and drink the cup, you proclaim the death of the Lord, until he comes.

1 Corinthians 11.23-26

70

Living God, host and guest,
we await you in the Household of Hope!
Come to us,
commune with us,
connect us;
and, as we break bread together,
make us true companions*
with all who seek for meaning and truth, beauty and love:
women and men; children and adults;
black and white; gay and straight;
unemployed and wage-earners;
uneducated and learned;
all who contribute to your Household's rich variety.
Come as provider and partaker:
come as our one and triune God,
that, in communion with you,
we may find community with each other.

* *Companions*: literally, those who eat bread together.

71

The fire is lit,
the table set,
the door stands open.
Come to eat and drink;
come to be part of this community;
come to be part of a world-wide communion
of those who trust in Jesus.

Come round the table,
saint and sinner,
stranger and friend,
to break bread,
to share wine
prepared and poured for you.

In sharing the symbols
of life-blood spilled
and body broken,
we become one with Christ,
and one with all those
who, hurting, yearn for healing today.

Come!
Here is food
for your healing,
bread and wine for your journey.
Come to be full-filled
by God,
the Giver and Lover of all.

72

God of holiness and love,
you are the unseen God
    yet you show yourself to the eyes of faith.
You are beyond our imagining
    yet you come as one of us that we might understand.
We give you thanks for this bread and wine:
    they represent the gifts of nature you have given us;
    they represent our offerings to you.
We thank you that you came in Jesus to set us free:
    in him we see your glory;
    in him we see your love and forgiveness;
    in him we see what we might become.
We give you thanks for this bread and wine:
    they remind us of your love;
    they remind us of your call to give ourselves.
We offer them in love.
We will take them in faithfulness.
We will receive them in thankfulness.

73

We have heard of one whose life and limbs were broken on a cross
yet still forgave and healed and loved.
Broken by life, and life's deep hurt
    we come to this table, searching for a source of health and wholeness.
Hopes shattered by the blows of unexpected circumstance,
    we come to this table, seeking a place of harmony and peace.
Leaving a trail of broken relationships we do not know how to mend,
    we come to this table longing for forgiveness and renewal.
Broken Christ, heal us.
Desolate Christ, give us hope.
Rejected Christ, renew us,
for only you can understand.

74 An invocation for three voices.

1 Who can sit at this table?
2 North and south; east and west;
3 Conservative and radical; liberal and charismatic;
2 European and Asian; American and Australian.

1 Who can join this community?
3 Black and white; orange and green;
2 Left and right; rich and poor;
3 Worker and manager; share-holder and customer.

1 Who can take this bread and wine?
2 Protestant and Catholic; Orthodox and Coptic;
3 Believer and searcher; enquirer and committed;
2 Young and old; strong and feeble.

1 Come! Come now! All things are ready;
The Lord has prepared the table for his people.

75

Broken man; Christ-crucified; poured-out life,
and all for us, so undeserving.
We come in poverty and loss
for we can bring no sacrifice except our praise.
We come in weakness and with uncertain steps
for we can bring no strength unless you take us by the arm.
We come in doubt and indecision
for we can bring no confidence until we see the welcome in your eyes.
We come with crippling sin, no merit in our hands
for we can bring no love unless you love us into love.

But still we come,
and come with hope,
for you have called, and you are true.
And so because we hear your gentle voice,
and trust you as we have before,
we come with lifted eyes and growing faith
to offer thanks
and speak our praise.

76

Can we, who every day
eat more than meets our need,
yet know of those
to whom bread is denied,
still come to this table
and take bread?

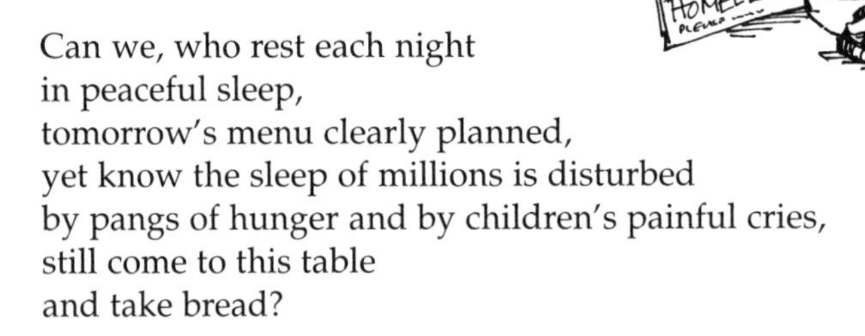

Can we, insulated in our ease,
and never visited by gnawing pain,
yet see and hear of those
daily assailed by hunger's grief,
still come to this table
and take bread?

Can we, who rest each night
in peaceful sleep,
tomorrow's menu clearly planned,
yet know the sleep of millions is disturbed
by pangs of hunger and by children's painful cries,
still come to this table
and take bread?

Can we, who come as beggars
to the table of the Lord,
yet know that others in their begging for their daily bread
are Government-denied and public-scorned,
and often too by us dismissed,
still come to this table
and take bread?

Yes, still we come,
and come we must:
    to confess our part in others' loss;
    to be challenged by the face of pain;
    to feel the shame of inequality;
and to give thanks,
yes thanks
that in our giving, prayers and work,
quick-born of love and love's demands,
we find a slender solidarity
with those who bear the burdens of our time,
and meet them here, unseen,
the welcome guests of our own Lord.

77

Let us give thanks
for humble and unassuming mediators
of the powerful grace of God,
and especially for the Servant Christ
and those who walk in his Way.
Let us give thanks
for the birth of Christ in an outhouse
to an ordinary couple, members of a despised nation;
for his growth in grace,
and learning of a humble trade.
Let us give thanks
for the fidelity of unsung disciples today
who offer hospitality to Christ in heart, home and work-place,
sharing his tears and his laughter,
offering their hands and feet as his in the world.
Calling God, we thank you;
For to shame the wise:
You have chosen what the world counts folly.
And to shame what is strong:
You have chosen what the world counts weakness.

Let us give thanks
for the teaching, healing and witness of Christ in a circumscribed world:
for his choice of fallible and weak vessels
to receive his wisdom and continue his work.
Let us give thanks
that still, today, he chooses unlikely people in unglamorous places
to realize his dreams and visions,
and express in their lives the buried, unheard secrets of God,
offering their ears and tongues as his in the world.
Calling God, we thank you;
For to shame the wise:
You have chosen what the world counts folly.
And to shame what is strong:
You have chosen what the world counts weakness.

Let us give thanks
for Christ's ignominious death outside a city wall,
and his dawn rising from a borrowed tomb:
for his first resurrection appearance to discounted women,
and his special concern for doubting Thomas.

Let us give thanks
for his bias, through the ages,
towards the poor and humble, the marginalized and questioning,
that the powerless might be dignified with Kingdom authority,
offering their own wounds as his to heal the world.
Calling God, we thank you;
  For to shame the wise:
  You have chosen what the world counts folly.
  And to shame what is strong:
  You have chosen what the world counts weakness.

Let us give thanks
for the down-to-earthness of bread and wine,
chosen by Christ to symbolize his body and his blood,
and for all ordinary and homely elements
that mediate the cascading grace of God.
Let us give thanks
for the divine audacity
which has always chosen things low and contemptible
to astound the wise and the powerful,
offering the passion of love to break and re-create the world.
For all these gifts, let us give thanks.

78

Lord, we lift our hearts to you:
thank you for life, its memory and hope;
thank you for growth, its challenge and renewal;
thank you for thought, its imagination and insight.
Our gratitude is rooted in your love for us
which you have made so clear in Jesus Christ.
Flesh and blood,
  he made love live.
Sowing the gift of love within our hearts
  he joined us to each other, and to you.
He called men and women to be his friends
and gave himself for them
as now for us.
He broke the bread and shared the cup
which we will take with gratitude,
his saving love made real within our hearts
as we become his body in the world.

79

We thank you, gracious God;
your Word did not come to us like a raging torrent
  sweeping us blindly along,
nor as a powerful earthquake
  bringing us to our knees in helpless terror.
No, you came like a glimpse of the sun in a darkening sky;
  like a green branch, unexpected in winter;
  like rain falling softly on the dry earth;
  like the first smile of a baby;
  the touch of a gentle lover.
So you came, gracious in coming,
and gracious yet in invitation.

You came as a child swaddling-wrapped and manger-held,
as a young man with question leading on to deeper question;
a teacher drawing out the truth we knew already
and crowning it with truth new-born and fresh.

Stripped of power and empty flourish
you came as a servant:
  kneeling, foot-washing;
  suffering in a suffering world;
  dying to bring life.

As a stranger by the seaside calling to adventure, so you came;
as a victim of injustice, a scapegoat of a sinning world;
a companion on a road, shy to reveal himself;
a gardener whispering the name of a long-loved friend.
And now you are not hidden from our sight;
with silent tread, through open door, through dust and joy, you come,
for you are one with us: Immanuel.

And are you now like bread held in our hands,
  a cup pressed to the lips?
And shall we see you in our neighbours' eyes,
  find you in each other's faith,
  and know your unseen presence as an open secret
as once again, mysteriously, but with so sure a touch and voice
you call us on to be your people in your world
and we pour out our thankful praise,
and take the bread, and drink the wine
as though they were your very self?

80 A prayer for two voices

1 Father God, you have never left us orphaned,
2 always you have offered yourself to us, sharing your love and your life.
1 You have never stopped searching for us,
2 always you have spoken your word to us,
offering forgiveness and comfort.
1 You have never stopped surprising us,
2 always you have found new ways of making your presence known
and seen.

1 We come to you, Lord, a forgetful people
but eager and longing to remember: to remember Jesus;
2 Jesus' body; Jesus' energy;
1 Jesus' blood; Jesus' cross;
2 Jesus the broken bread; Jesus the crushed grapes.
1 We come to you remembering how much we are in your debt
2 for you alone love to the end,
you alone forgive until it hurts,
you alone face Pilate and the crowd,
and see it through to the end.
1 We come remembering how little we have learned through the centuries:
2 how little ...
1 about power,
2 about peace,
1 about selfishness,
2 about hope,
1 about ourselves,
2 and about you.
1 We remember you in this moment, O God,
because we do these things in remembrance of Jesus, your Son.
The bread and wine are a sign of your presence and your victory.
2 Risen bread, glorious grapes.

1 Thank you, Jesus, for your body, bound for the cross,
2 but then let loose in the world.
1 Thank you, Jesus, for your blood, poured out in pain,
2 but later to be the life-stream of your people.
1 Thank you for our friends here whom we serve.
2 Thank you for being our Lord, serving us here.
1 Thank you for your sharing.
2 Thank you for your daring.
1 Thank you for this meal.
1 & 2 Hear this our prayer, Jesus.
In your name we offer it.

81

Holy God,
for the universe you have made
in all its variety and mystery; **We praise and thank you.**

For the gift of your beloved Son,
vulnerable healer; **We praise and thank you.**

For your work of salvation,
love crucified and victorious; **We praise and thank you.**

With all people everywhere,
past, present and yet to come; **We praise and thank you.**

That you have brought us together around this table,
no longer strangers but pilgrims,
companions on a journey; **We praise and thank you.**

Send your Spirit of faith, hope and love
on us now,
and on this bread and wine
that, sharing them,
we may become your living body,
active in your world.

82

Lord Jesus Christ,
you are for us our bread of life,
as vulnerable as bread placed in the hand,
to be accepted with joy or cast aside;
as satisfying as bread to the hungry,
and giving life for the future;
broken like bread before all can share,
and as necessary as bread to sustain our living.

Lord Jesus Christ, you are for us our spiritual drink;
rich as the blood-red, sun-filled grape,
taken, pressed and destroyed to new-create;
welcome as the clean, fresh draught to the weary traveller,
drawn from the deep, clear well that never fails;
gift to our thirst to meet our need,
poured out in love that all might share.
Bread and wine you are; food and drink – to our eternal satisfaction.

83

What we have seen and heard, touched and tasted,
here, within these walls,
we take with us into the wider community,
and there make known
the power of the Creator,
the love of the Liberator
and the peace of the Reconciler.

84

As bread is broken for the world,
may we feel the world's brokenness.

As we share bread with others,
may we share our time and money.
  Make us good stewards
  of what we leave in our pockets,
  as well as accountable for what we give.
In our common life,
may we remember the God of creation,
the mothering, enfolding, naming God;
the God who never abandons us.

As wine is poured out for the world,
may we feel the world's pain.

As we share the cup of suffering
with our neighbour,
may we also share our experience.
  Make us good stewards of opportunity;
  to listen, to confront, to work
  for healing, peace and community.
In our common life,
may we remember the God of redemption,
the saving, salving, suffering God;
the God who never forgets us.

Thanks be to God
whose body was broken on a wooden cross
to bring all things into perfect unity,
and to the Spirit whose wings bring healing,
and whose presence spells peace.

85

As you have been fed at this table,
go to feed the hungry.
As you have been set free,
go and release the imprisoned.
As you have received – give.
As you have heard – proclaim.
And the blessing
which you have received
from Father, Son and Holy Spirit
be always with you.

86

Like grapes on a sun-drenched hill
we, who came as individuals,
are now made one,
abiding in Christ
who dwells in us.
Our thirst is quenched,
the bread of life has filled us.
May we leave this table
restored and committed
to serve with justice
the thirsty and the empty
with whom we are now one body.

In the name of Christ;
bread-giver
and strengthener.

87

Encircle us with your power;
encompass us with your grace;
embrace your dying ones;
support your weary ones;
calm your frightened ones
and, as the sun scatters the mist on the hills,
bring us to a new dawn
when all shall freely sit at table
in your Kingdom,
rejoicing in a God who saves his people.

88

God of travail,
at one with Mary in pregnancy and birth,
and nailed to humankind upon the cross;
in our eating this day
we have been consumed again by your mystery among us.

God of laughter,
welcoming strangers,
joining the dance of children;
in our drinking this day
the music of your banquet rings out among us.

God of justice,
struggling in the lives of the poor,
wrongly accused,
falsely imprisoned;
the vision of justice, hope and integrity is on our breath and in our bones.

God of surprises,
we who have eaten bread and drunk wine
wonder
and wait.

89

Lord, we have seen your promised victory.
Let it lead us
not to world-renouncing piety,
nor to self-righteous condemnation,
but to an ever stronger conviction that you are calling out
a transformed creation,
a genesis renewed,
through the power of the Lamb that was slain.

Remind us that the pain of the world
is gathered up into a new heaven and earth,
not through divine magic
but through the mystery of the incarnation:
I will make my home among you. You will be my people; I will be your God.
For this, our praise resounds
throughout the universe,
world without end.

90

In the beginning – one God, one world.
In the lives of patriarchs, poets and prophets – one vision, one world.
In Jesus Christ – one goal, one Lord.
In the end – one people, one Kingdom
for ever and ever.

91

Living God,
with all your saints
past, present and future,
we proclaim the victory of your Kingdom.
We commit ourselves
to the Easter task
of bringing your glorious future
into our inglorious present.
Then shall your Spirit
so fill our today
that the world will see the joy of the blessed ones,
enabling its past to be forgiven
and its future to be placed in your hands,
through Jesus Christ
the same yesterday, today and for ever.

92

Living God, host and guest,
you have been present with us in this Household of Hope!
You have come to us,
communed with us,
connected us;
and, as we broke bread together,
we were companions
with saints past and present,
those near and dear to us, and those now far away.
You have been with us as provider and partaker;
and now, as you send us out again,
may we take our worship into your world,
your stillness into all our speaking and doing,
and our communion with you here into the search for true community
with one another and all your creatures.

Vestry Prayers

Lord of Hosts,
how dearly loved is your dwelling-place!

I pine and faint with longing
for the courts of the Lord's temple;
my whole being cries out with joy
to the living God.

Even the sparrow finds a home,
and the swallow has her nest
where she rears her brood beside your altars,
Lord of Hosts, my King and God.

Happy are those who dwell in your house;
they never cease to praise you!

Psalm 84.1-4

93

To you, our God,
be all the glory, the honour, the praise.
From you, our God,
be our assurance of your presence amongst us.
Bless our time together in worship,
and bless us as we go out in service,
that all we do, and all we are
is to do your will, and be your people.
In Jesus' name.

94

O God,
may this place and this hour
be the arena in which
we truly meet you, acknowledge you, hear and respond to you.
And through encountering you in your holiness,
may we thereby also meet, acknowledge, hear and respond to one another
more authentically and more lovingly
here and hereafter.

95

What privilege to serve in the sanctuary of praise!
How weighty the burden of leadership of your people in worship!
Bless all charged with ministry amongst us today – in pulpit and pew –
that through the preaching of the Word
and the caring fellowship of the faithful,
we all may find our faith deepened
and our mission made more clear.
In Jesus' name.

96

Grant us peace, Lord;
your people wait upon you in quietness.
Give us inner serenity, Lord;
your people stand in need of renewal.
Bring us to unity, Lord;
your people would worship you in harmony.

97

Listening God,
may worship happen here today
not just in outward form
but in spirit and in truth.
Come, Holy Spirit,
open our eyes,
unstop our ears,
expand our minds,
gladden our hearts and give them wings,
that we may know with our whole being
that Christ is in our midst.

98

God,
you have given us this day,
unique and precious,
for re-creation and renewal.
Help us to receive it as a gift
in which we can hear you speaking to us
and to the world:
  words of promise and fulfilment;
  words of encouragement and support;
  words of challenge and judgement;
  words of love and forgiveness.
Use our voices and minds
to help this congregation to worship
in spirit and in truth,
to the glory of Jesus Christ, our Lord.

99

Let us keep silence
as we prepare to worship the God
who is deep within us
and all around us.
  Silence
May our worship
touch the hearts and minds of all,
giving glory to God
through Christ,
our brother.

100 God,
present,
available,
active,
welcoming;
there is no place
where you are absent,
there is no heart
you cannot touch,
there is no situation
beyond your transforming Spirit.
Help us to worship you this day
with sincerity and energy,
giving in leadership
the best we can offer,
but throughout the experience
expecting you to lead us
into the surprises
of your Kingdom,
through Jesus,
our Lord.

101 Living God, through this worship
unite our spirits
  to rise on the wings of the morning;
make our minds buzz
  with the excitement of hearing the gospel;
renew our commitment
  through the fellowship of the Spirit;
and equip us to be your people in the world
  acting in the name of Jesus.

102 Spirit of God,
uplift those who will lead our worship today;
guide all who seek to inspire us through music and words.
Spirit of God,
move among the congregation today,
generating praise and repentance,
renewal and rededication.

Spirit of God,
go with us when we leave,
so that the pattern of our worship
becomes a pattern for our living.
In the name of Jesus Christ.

103 Lord, as we get ready to go into church,
take the planning and preparation,
take the resources of hymn-book and Bible,
take the faith of the church, and our personal discipleship,
take the experiences of this past week,
take our constant hopes and perpetual fears,
and weave them together with the threads of your Spirit
into an act of worship
which will honour you
and equip us.

104 As the people of God gather for worship, we pray for each member of the congregation, that we may bring all that we are – our pleasures and our regrets – to God.
Father, as we sing, pray and reflect together, may we offer you the worship you deserve and be renewed for your service.
We pray for those who will lead our worship. May their words become your words so that your people can worship with joy and commitment.

105 Father, today you have given us
a time to meet together,
a time to celebrate your love,
a time to share one another's joys and sorrows,
a time to build each other up,
a time to explore our faith in Jesus,
and a time to be equipped to serve you.
Help us to use this time for our good
and your glory.

106 This day, O God,
may our lips sing out in praise,
our eyes be opened to see your glory,
our ears be alert to hear your word,
and our hearts be filled with your love,
so that in worship we can give to you,
and also receive from you,
great and wonderful God.

107 Lord, now take from our minds all that intrudes
and prevents us from worshipping you:
  our worries of the past week;
  our random thoughts of things to come;
  our irritation at the choice of hymns;
  our complacency in our own ability;
  our concern for what others think of us.
Fill our hearts with love for you alone
so that we can focus our whole being on worshipping you,
and giving you all praise and honour, truly deserved.

108 Gather us, O God,
that we may come
expectant to worship,
bringing with us
the pain and joy
of the week that is past.
  Grant that what we do
  in your name
  may be done
  to your glory,
  that justice and peace
  may embrace,
  love and faith unite.

109

If the Lord's disciples keep silent these stones would shout aloud.

Lord, in our praise
and in our prayer,
in our listening
and in our speaking,
may singer and song,
speaker and hearer
become part
of the ongoing worship
of your eternal praise.

110

God, Creator, Enfolder, Sustainer,
we come to you at the start of a new week.
We come to you bringing our joys and sorrows.
We come to you, knowing that your fingerprint
is on each soul;
that you have carved our names
in the hollow of your hand.

God, Creator of the galaxies,
nearer to us than hands and feet,
we come to worship you.

Silence

Jesus says: those who come to me I will not cast out ...

Silence

Holy Spirit, Encourager,
come to us.
Fill our worship
with your power and your love;
in the name of the Creator,
the Redeemer
and the Sustainer.

The Church Community

It is through faith that you are all sons of God in union with Christ Jesus. Baptized into union with him, you have all put on Christ like a garment. There is no such thing as Jew and Greek, slave and freeman, male and female; for you are all one person in Christ Jesus.

Galatians 3.26-28

If then our common life in Christ yields anything to stir the heart, any consolation of love, any participation in the Spirit, any warmth of affection or compassion, fill up my cup of happiness by thinking and feeling alike, with the same love for one another and a common attitude of mind. Leave no room for selfish ambition and vanity, but humbly reckon others better than yourselves. Look to each other's interests and not merely to your own.

Philippians 2.1-4

111 Living God,
you have promised your presence
where two or three
come together to worship you with sincerity.

Wherever a community gathers like this
you are actually there;
silently, invisibly,
but truly.
What a miracle of love and grace!

You don't demand a crowd;
you seek a group of friends.

Help us to be that for you
and for each other
this day.
Then speak to us –
words of comfort,
and words to disturb us;
heal us of division and pain,
and raise us to new commitment.
Remind us of all you have done,
and challenge us to continue your work
to the glory of Jesus Christ, our Lord.

112 We come as a gathered group of your people, Lord God, to give and to receive. We come with hearts moved to give praise and to receive hope. We come with lives moved to give service and to receive a sense of purpose. As we gather, we pray that we may know you near. Bless this time we share, that in our giving we may receive, and in our receiving we may know your will, and in the knowing we may fulfil our calling as part of your world-wide family of faith. This we pray in the name and for the sake of Jesus Christ.

113 We are your people, loving God,
by the grace of your calling:
chosen and precious,
picked for Christ's sake;
called to service,
part of the world-wide Church.

As we gather for worship,
we pray that we may know
the persistent power
of your Spirit's presence amongst us.
In Christ's name we meet and pray.

114 Heavenly Father,
how glad we are to come to church:
to sing and pray,
to learn and teach,
to offer adoration and praise,
to meet our friends and greet newcomers.
And more:
to tell you with sadness of our sins, and seek forgiveness,
to grieve for the hurt in the world, and acknowledge our part in it.

Now, as we offer such thoughts, we pause
to remember your Church throughout the world
and know afresh how your people in every place
share our gladness and sadness.
For even as we speak,
beneath the African sun your name is blessed,
across the broad plains of Australia the voice of prayer is raised,
in the teeming cities of India songs of praise are sung,
beneath the snow-clad mountains of Austria and Switzerland
the Church rejoices.
Other places can be mentioned, especially where the local church has contacts.
And more;
for some Christians worship, fearful of persecution,
others almost engulfed by alien creeds,
some risk livelihood and home as they confess that Christ is Lord,
and others must choose between their family and their Lord.

Heavenly Father,
how glad we are to come to church, and how full of prayer and hope
for the world-wide Church of Jesus Christ.

115 Loving God, present throughout the world you have made,
we come to you in a time set aside for worship;
for thinking your thoughts, breathing in time with your Spirit,
and walking in step with your purpose.
Your whole Church across the world worships you!

Our worship comes with mingled joy and sadness,
for we worship you in a world
where some children dance each day with joy and delight,
and others daily weep with sadness;
where some families live in loving unity,
and others live lives broken and disjointed;
where some nations war and feed on oppression,
and others learn to create community and harmony;
a world where you are known, honoured and loved by many,
and spurned, despised or ignored by others.

All-seeing God, in such a world we live,
in such a world we believe in justice, love and peace,
in such a world we will proclaim the good news to all peoples,
and in such a world we worship you;
for in such a world we know that you are present in every part;
known or unknown, loved or ignored,
and you always will be.

All-knowing God,
though your Church speaks out across the world this day in praise,
we come also in the spirit of confession and regret.
We are ashamed of so much that happens in the world
but acknowledge that your sinful Church has contributed to its downfall.
We grieve that there is so much darkness in the world
but confess that your Church has not always been a beacon of light.
We long for a wholesome, united world
but know that your Church has played a part in its brokenness
and despair.

Ever-loving God, forgive us.
Grant that your Church may be so renewed by worship this day,
so uplifted by your presence
and so united in its ministry and mission to the ends of the earth,
that we become agents of the life of the Kingdom,
and share with you in the re-creation of human society
in the name of Jesus Christ, our Lord.

116 Gracious, patient God,
you must have wept
again and again
at the failures of congregations like ours.

You must have wept
at our lack of vision.
Yet you still ask us to speak for you.

You must have wept
over our apathy and indifference.
Yet you still give us your living Spirit.

You must have wept
at our inconsistency.
Yet you still show us opportunities to serve.

You must have wept
at our pessimism and grumbling.
Yet you still provide us with good news.

You must have wept
at our disunity and division.
Yet you still call us to be friends.

You must have wept
at the impoverishment of our worship.
Yet you still receive our prayers and praises.

Why are you so patient?
Why do you still love us?

Is it because Jesus never stopped loving his friends to the end
and pleads for us now?

Is it because that is the way you are
and the way you have always been?
You keep the covenant.
You restore our souls.
You still seek to lead us in the paths of righteousness.

117 Lord, you made the world and everything in it;
you created one human race, of one stock,
and in your loving purpose
you gave us the earth for our possession.
Forgive us for breaking what you created whole,
and dividing what you intended as a unity.
Father in heaven: **Show us the unity of your earth again.**

Forgive us our secret delight that the oceans divide the nations
as though love could not build bridges.
Father in heaven: **Show us the unity of your earth again.**

Forgive us when we take refuge in patriotic nationalism
as though you had not made us one race, one people.
Father in heaven: **Show us the unity of your earth again.**

Forgive us when we speak of the rainbow colours of the human face
and then live monochrome lives.
Father in heaven: **Show us the unity of your earth again.**

Forgive us when we use the variety of languages as an excuse for silence
as though we could not learn a language other than our mother-tongue.
Father in heaven: **Show us the unity of your earth again.**

Forgive us when we think the clothes and dress of other nations quaint
and forget the varying fashions in our own cities and towns.
Father in heaven: **Show us the unity of your earth again.**

Forgive us when we allow ourselves to be shocked by warring nations abroad
and ignore the sharp divisions in our own land.
Father in heaven: **Show us the unity of your earth again.**

Make us glad when we are challenged:
by new ideas and places as we travel;
by different cultures as we hear from friends far distant;
by new insights into your purposes as we meet with partner churches;
by television as the joy and sadness of other nations enters our homes;
and by the growing conviction that as we listen, learn and read
you show us the unity of your earth again.

118 Merciful God, we rejoice that you entered the world in Jesus Christ.
We rejoice that looking to Christ we see you, and so we know you as love:
not soft and sentimental love,
but love that looses the shackles of sinfulness and promises a better way.
Forgive us when we fail:
as individuals, falling short of your glory;
and together as your Church, when we hurt each other
and frustrate your purposes.
Forgive us that we fail to value each person's presence amongst us
as the gift from you it is.
Forgive us, and teach us how to build each other up in the truth of the gospel
and the fellowship of faith,
for the sake of Jesus Christ.

119 Loving God,
you call each of us to ministry,
giving to each congregation
a variety and richness
which we often take for granted.

Accept our thanks
for each person present here today,
no matter their age or background.

Accept our thanks
for the gifts they bring
to the whole body of the Church, creating enrichment and health.

Accept our thanks
for the faithfulness of countless people
who have never stopped worshipping,
even when they have been hurt by the Church,
or were angry with life.
Accept our thanks
that they put loyalty to you above all else,
and did not let their own emotions
get in the way of their faithfulness.

Accept our thanks also, Lord,
for those who have been the Church's disturbers:
  defending the marginalized;
  stopping us from being inward-looking;
  searching for the truth ardently but lovingly.

Accept our thanks
for children and grown-ups
who have not held back when asked to serve:
those willing people who have been loyal to a task
which they only took on for a short time,
but which became a long commitment of time and energy.

Accept our thanks
for all who have offered gifts of leadership:
  ministers of the word and sacraments,
  elders, stewards, musicians, deacons,
  pastoral workers and teachers.

But, Lord, our greatest thanks is for all faithful Christians
who have been clothed in joy,
wrapped in humility,
shining examples of the way Jesus
spoke, healed, taught and served,
for these are the saints of today;
a wonderful gift from you to the world.

120 Eternal God, with all who have gone before us in the faith,
we praise your name.
With all across the world, in every land,
with peoples of every race, colour and tongue,
we sing your praise.
With the whole creation:
  mountain and hill, wood and forest,
  sea and stream, sun, moon and stars,
we proclaim your greatness.
We unite with all that is past, all around us,
and all that is yet to be
so that with creation in its completeness,
we acknowledge you as Lord.

121 Loving God,
we give you thanks for our church.
Sadly we confess that we so often fail:
we turn from tasks you give us;
we shrink from speaking out our faith;
we shy away from mission.
Yet gladly we recognize that we meet with some success:
sometimes we get things right;
sometimes we declare our faith with clarity;
sometimes we turn our time and talents to the mission you give us.

We can barely begin
to shoulder the responsibility
of being your Church in your world;
but you choose to make no other plan
but that your Word be known through us.
We thank you for that privilege
and for the times
when others catch the excitement of our faith
and are drawn onto the path of pilgrimage
through words said and love shown through your Church.

Loving God, thanking you for the Church,
we pray for its continuing effectiveness
as a witness to the glorious good news of the gospel.
In Jesus' name.

122 Thanks be to you, loving God, for what you have done for the whole world in Jesus Christ, your Son. On our behalf he died. For our sakes, he bore the punishment of sin. And we are reprieved. Guilt no longer crushes us for, as we turn and ask, so you forgive.

We thank you that in Christ you reconciled the world to yourself and, despite our inadequacy, have entrusted the ministry of reconciliation to us. Your Church is priest and pastor to the world. By your call we embody your purpose, proclaim your will, and take good news to those who need to know.

Loving God, thank you for the trust you show in us: bearing your blessing to pauper and prince, touching lives forlorn with the hope of renewal, proclaiming the gospel to every nation, and completing joy in those hearts already filled with praise.

Thank you for the purpose you give us: making your grace known, pointing to your will and nurturing your ways in the world you have always loved.

We pray that we may serve faithfully, supporting one another in the church in the tasks you give us to do; for the sake of those for whom you call us to care; in Christ's name.

123

Thank you, living God,
for the potent hope of the good news of the gospel
reaching out to the ends of the earth:
  renewing lives burned by guilt and sorrow;
  redeeming lives puffed up in pride;
  resurrecting lives drowned in confusion, doubt or despair;
  fulfilling lives lost from love, purpose or direction;
  completing joy
  and shedding new light into dark days.

Thank you that you are seldom silent,
and that your silence speaks louder than words.
Thank you that your voice speaks through people, scripture and circumstance,
making your will known to souls hungry to hear and thirsty to know.

Above all, thank you for Jesus Christ.
He is the perfect reflection of your love for the world.
He is your very self amongst us.
He is our very self in our nakedness.
In him we know hope,
through him we find salvation,
and by him we are embraced by you.

Thank you for the Church, called by Christ,
and built to reflect your grace, mercy, challenge, justice, and love for the world.
Thank you for your faithful servants in all places and of all times,
guided and gifted by you to make the faith known
and build the Church in the world, for the world.
For ourselves we pray: that we may be faithful to speak out the truths we have received, and never shrink from declaring the hope that is in us.
In Christ's name we pray, and for his sake.

124 O Christ,
does a mother stop
from stooping and sifting the rubbish
in a South American rubbish tip –
    stop and listen to the songbird
    and know that the pain which pierces her heart
    is your pain?

O Christ,
does a child stop
from hustling and haggling the punters
on the pavements of Brazil –
    stop and look at the stars
    and know that the hunger in his belly
    is your hunger?

O Christ,
does a young girl stop
from walking and working the streets
in the suburbs of the cities –
    stop and enjoy the scent of a flower
    and know that the anger in her heart
    is your anger?

O Christ,
does an old man stop
from carrying and cursing the water
in the polluted wastes of Iraq –
    stop and feel the wind on his face
    and know that his thirst
    is your thirst?

Lord, help your Church to hear
your song of praise
in the cry of the hungry and thirsty,
in the despair of the powerless.
And hearing, help us to act justly,
serve wisely and love prayerfully.
In your name and for your sake.

125 Living God,
you have set the Church in the world
as a sign of your Kingdom.
Each local Christian group
is like a star in your universe,
a lamp in the sky,
a brilliant sign of your presence.

We pray for these twinkling lights:
thousands of them,
each in their own particular place,
each separate, yet part of the galaxy of light.

We pray for those which are struggling:
where energy is sapped
and where vision is clouded;
for churches facing division,
and those wounded by internal strife.

We pray for those battered by outside forces:
churches persecuted by the surrounding community;
churches in areas of violence and fear;
churches attacked by military or political leaders;
churches facing financial and economic hardship.

We pray for churches which are despondent:
churches lacking in leadership;
congregations facing tragic personal situations;
churches depleted in numbers and resources;
small congregations in remote villages, or in inner-city ghettos.

We pray for churches which are alive and growing,
that they may not pander to popularity
or forget to be sacrificial to their neighbourhoods.
May strong churches help weaker ones,
and strength be measured not in numbers
but in faithfulness to your Gospel.

God of the universal Church,
all these are lights in your Kingdom.
May they shine with your glory, reflect your purpose
and be a credit to your name for ever and ever.

126 Bless your Church, loving God!
May it express its devotion to you
in ways that move hearts and minds
to follow Christ
and serve as he directs all the days of our lives.

Bless your Church, loving God!
May it show you to be our seven-day-a-week God:
forever present,
forever caring,
forever ready to hear the prayers of your people.

Bless your Church, loving God!
May it share fellowship that breaks barriers;
display sacrifice at its heart;
rejoice in its unity of purpose
and welcome its diversity of people.

We pray for the world.
We pray that the fellowship of the Church
will stand as a sign of the possibility of barrier-breaking.

We pray for those individuals in our world
who never know the supporting strength of loving fellowship;
whose lives are lonely, and whose hope is dim.

We pray for those who meet face to face with urgent human need
and seek to bring comfort and strength
to peoples disregarded and forgotten;
casting light into darkness, hope into despair,
and resurrecting life from the ashes of sorrow.

We offer these prayers
in the name and for the sake of Jesus Christ.

127 We rejoice that the Church is
no mere huddle of the holy,
no simple gathering of the pious,
no exclusive club of the convinced,
but a living, vital community reaching to the ends of the earth.

We rejoice, living God,
that the Church is not a dinosaur
preserved only for its past,
but a living, breathing blessing for the present,
and a hope for the future.

We rejoice that the faith we seek, the faith we hold, the faith we profess,
is no dead document of outdated precepts,
but a vibrant and saving perspective on life today
in all its rainbow colours, all its splendid glory.

We rejoice that the gospel
is everywhere and at all times relevant:
bringing purpose and direction to lives;
bringing renewal to the forlorn;
bringing light to those in darkness;
bringing the aspect of eternity to our everyday and ordinary.
In Christ's name we rejoice.
In Christ's name we pray.

128 Almighty God,
you ever call people
to worship you and serve you
in village, town and city.
Enable these churches to be living communities of faith:
resourced by your Spirit,
equipped to serve,
active in neighbourhood care,
eager to be open and welcoming,
anxious to be in partnership with others,
courageous in coming alongside the poor and lonely,
ready to weep with the sad,
  celebrate with the joyful,
  carry the burdens of the guilty,
  and be loving to all.

Be glorified,
we pray,
in faithful, sincere worship
wherever it is created and offered.

Be glorified
in deeds of forgiveness and commitment
wherever your saints serve boldly.

Be glorified
where children praise and young people question,
where adults grow in experience,
and old people donate their wisdom.

Be glorified
where life is given away,
where neighbourhoods are resurrected,
and the wounds of society are touched and healed.

Be glorified
where people of different traditions and backgrounds
forget past divisions,
and come together in a spirit of unity and trust.
Be glorified in us
today and always.

We ask it in Jesus' name.

129 Gracious God, we pray that people will see the sacrificial life of Christ in the life of the Church: the willingness to give of its life-blood so that light and life become known in dark and barren places.

We pray that we may become the body of Christ in deed as well as word: sharing the loads of misery and doubt, uncertainty, confusion and sadness in the world.

We pray that your Church becomes a channel for your healing grace, upbuilding faith and strengthening fellowship. In Christ's name.

130 We pray that the Church in every land be marked:
with Christian unity in loving fellowship,
and common hope shown to the world.

We pray that the Church in every place be faithful:
that the marginalized, rejected and forgotten
become embraced in its mission,
and the complacent and comfortable
are challenged with others' need.

We pray that the Church in every village and town be vocal:
telling out the gospel,
speaking words of healing,
talking truth for life.

In the name and for the sake of Jesus Christ,
who called the Church into being.

131 Lord Jesus,
where your Church is wealthy among the poor,
fearful in the midst of injustice,
cowardly among the oppressed,
give us, we pray,
  new confidence in your Kingdom,
  new hope in your purpose,
  new faith in your power,
  and new trust in your nearness.
Then turn our wealth, our fear and even our cowardice
into resources of strength
to serve your people
in your name.

132 From the corners of the world,
From the loneliness of our hearts,
From the confusion of life,
Gather us, O God.

To feed our minds,
To fire our imagination,
To free our hearts,
Gather us, O God.

133 Reconciling God,
we come as old and young, male and female,
black and white, employed and unemployed,
and with differing degrees of disability.
We come with Christians far and near
and discover the unity we have in Christ.
Father, Son and Spirit: Holy Trinity,
you draw us into your communion of love.
Make us more than a society, having things in common.
Make us more than neighbours, linked by a place in common.
Build us into a community; companions with you in sharing your love.
Be with us as we worship, healing hurt and discord,
and creating a dynamic harmony of praise.

134 Loving Father God,
we come as one family to worship you.
Young and old,
we come as one family to worship you.
With agile step or slow,
we come as one family to worship you.
Some of us have known you for a long time;
some of us are just beginning to learn of your love;
but, travellers together along Christ's way,
we come as one family to worship you.
O God of past and present and future,
always the same, yet always new;
O God and Father of us all,
we come as one family to worship you.

135 Lord,
When we look into the face
of someone we know and love,
we see them as they are:
    wise, kind or funny,
    stubborn, grumpy or sad,
    and understand and accept them.
But, Lord,
When we look into the face of strangers
we see young or old,
    male or female,
    wrinkles or spots,
    and rely on our first impressions.

Lord, you look into the hearts of people;
lovingly you know your children inside out, through and through.
Help us to learn to know one another lovingly,
with sensitivity and understanding.
May we value what each person can give us,
    enjoying their company,
    supporting them in their weakness,
    forgiving their shortcomings,
that we too might know and be able to accept them in love,
and thus learn afresh
your loving forgiveness of us all.
In the name of Christ our Saviour.

136 God our Healer,
in sorrow and shame
we bring you our brokenness,
that you may touch, forgive and heal.

We bring you
the cracks and chips in our most important relationships:
the misunderstandings and hurts we engender
in our families, between friends and lovers.

We bring you
the fissures and fractures in our worshipping communities:
the petty rivalries, our avoidance of real meeting;
the intolerance of difference, our wrong priorities.

We bring you
the shards and fragments of your wider household:
nations and cultures at war – or striving for supremacy;
the earth, exploited for gain, dying for want of our respect.

Where there is no vision, the people break loose.
Give us, we pray, dreams to bind and inspire us for the future,
hearts to forgive one another for the past,
and hands open to one another in the present.

137

How can we seek the warm safety of worship,
when so many are lonely and afraid?

O loving God,
help us to find worship to be
a sending and strengthening,
not to seek it
as an escape from reality.

For expecting too much,
for expecting too little,
good Lord, forgive us.

For making easy promises
and failing to keep them,
good Lord, forgive us.

For hasty words and thoughtless actions,
for easy answers and careless thinking,
good Lord, forgive us.

For avoiding the hurt of the world
and ignoring the needs of others,
good Lord, forgive us.

Those who seek shall find.
Those who ask for forgiveness
are forgiven.

138 Living, loving Lord of faith,
Thank you!
You welcome us all despite our differences.
When togetherness overcomes division – thank you.
When understanding dissolves stereotypes – thank you.
When human friendship offers support and challenge – thank you.
When quietness affirms your presence with us and within us – thank you.
For these, the gifts of your Spirit, thank you, living, loving Lord of faith.

139 O God of all youth, we pray to you.
We want to celebrate life,
life before death.
With the hungry and the unemployed,
with the homeless, the oppressed and the sick
we cry out to you.
Lord, in your mercy: **Hear our prayer.**

Lord of all history,
make new the places ravished by war.
Renew the peoples whose hopes have been destroyed.
Build up communities divided by suspicion.
Reconcile families broken apart by misunderstanding.
Lord, in your mercy: **Hear our prayer.**

Trinity of love, One God in perfect community,
hear the prayers of your children.
Let them come to you,
with all that hurts and disturbs them.
Welcome them with your healing smile.
Encircle them with your strong arms,
and send them out to serve you in your world.
Lord, in your mercy: **Hear our prayer.**

Adapted from a prayer written by a group of young people from Brazil

140 *'... the Church is meant to be: a laboratory of peace, a parable of the Kingdom, a sign of contradiction among the nations, a place of welcome amidst the sectarianism and xenophobia of the surrounding society, a community of praise ...'*

Brother Leonard of Taizé

Our God, you call us to be Church: enable us to create – across cultural, age and class boundaries – a laboratory of peace, testing out your vision of community and love as we struggle to live with our differences.

Our God, you call us to be Church: enable us to be a parable of the Kingdom, allowing the upside-down values of your commonwealth to nudge us away from the acquisitive and self-regarding attitudes of our day.

Our God, you call us to be Church: enable us to be a sign of contradiction among the nations, pointing to hope in the midst of disillusion, offering non-violent resistance when evil threatens, accepting loss of prestige or wealth in the cause of justice.

Our God, you call us to be Church: enable us to be a place of welcome and warmth, where what is ignored elsewhere may be heard and honoured, where sorrows may be shared and our stories told, where hard questions may be asked and new ideas greeted with joy.

Our God, you call us to be Church: enable us to be a community of praise, cracking open the dry husks of cynicism and despair, being clowns and jesters for Christ, celebrating the mystery of faith in stillness and song.

141 Lord, as we grow older, help us to remember
That you are always there beside us,
Enfolding, supporting, uplifting us
With your love.

We pray for those whose old age
Is a time of freedom and opportunity,
Asking that they might use their days well,
Living lovingly, joyfully,
And in celebration of their true selves.

We pray for those whose old age
Is a time of limitation and frustration,
Asking that they might know the inner freedom
That your Spirit alone can bring,
Your Spirit of love and comfort, of joy and peace.

We pray for those whose old age
Is richly peopled by family and friends,
Asking that they might be a source of strength
To those tossed by life's tempests,
Beacons of warm loving in dark times.

We pray for those whose old age
Is a time of loneliness and grief,
Asking that they might know God's loving presence,
Meeting him in the face of those caring for them,
Talking with him in their darkest hours.

Lord, as we grow older,
Life may become harder;
There are trials to face.
Help us to remember
That you are always there beside us,
Enfolding, supporting, uplifting us
With your love.

142 We affirm the glory of God's creation
and the potential for growth in all people.
We affirm our belief in Christ
as friend and brother.
We affirm the creative energy of the Spirit
awakening goodness, breaking down barriers.

We commit ourselves
to working with young people;
encouraging their gifts,
enabling their participation,
safeguarding their interests.

We commit ourselves
to supporting each other;
to walking alongside
the doubting and the downcast,
listening, not interfering.

We commit ourselves
to confronting superficial solutions,
speaking, not avoiding.

We commit ourselves
to rejoicing with those who rejoice,
to weeping with those who weep,
to being partners with those who serve.

We commit ourselves,
our time, energy and skills
as (youth) workers
in Christ's name, and for his sake.

143

'To garden with others is an expression of solidarity.'

Marta Benavides

We commit ourselves to the tasks of gardening –
that we may be a fruitful community
whose variety, harmony and secret growth in grace
may please our Creator God.

Together, we shall prepare the ground –
turning and lifting and sifting,
inviting the Spirit to aerate impacted soil –
enriching the garden of the People of God
with our prayers and quiet expectancy.

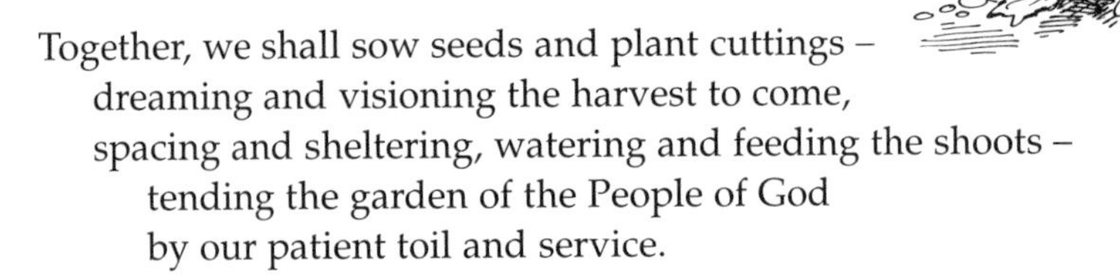

Together, we shall sow seeds and plant cuttings –
dreaming and visioning the harvest to come,
spacing and sheltering, watering and feeding the shoots –
tending the garden of the People of God
by our patient toil and service.

Together, we shall nurture the plants' growth –
rejoicing in the rich variety of colour and texture,
seeing how each complements the others,
allowing all to breathe, to drink, to blossom –
offering the garden of the People of God
as the first-fruits of justice-making in the garden of the world.

Mission and Ministry

... 'Everyone who calls on the name of the Lord will be saved.' But how could they call on him without having faith in him? And how could they have faith without having heard of him? And how could they hear without someone to spread the news? And how could anyone spread the news without being sent? As scripture says, 'How welcome are the feet of the messengers of good news!'

Romans 10.13-15

With this in mind, then, I kneel in prayer to the Father, from whom every family in heaven and on earth takes its name, that out of the treasures of his glory he may grant you inward strength and power through his Spirit, that through faith Christ may dwell in your hearts in love. With deep roots and firm foundations may you, in company with all God's people, be strong to grasp what is the breadth and length and height and depth of Christ's love, and to know it, though it is beyond knowledge. So may you be filled with the very fullness of God.

Ephesians 3.14-19

144 Gracious and eternal God,
maker, redeemer and inspirer,
we are your people;
you are our God.
We stand in line
with those you call to bear your love
to hungry souls.
And so we come,
within this place
to worship and to learn:
to offer praise;
to hear your word;
to do your will –
in the cause of your Kingdom,
and for the sake of your Son,
Jesus Christ our Lord.

145 Loving God,
we pray that we may know your Spirit in us and amongst us
as we gather for worship:
to offer our praise to you;
to seek to know your will for us;
to grow in faith and understanding,
and so to live out in actions
day by day
the faith we now proclaim in words.

146 Gracious God,
calling people to service
and risking their rejection,
we rejoice in the faithful response
of all who have heard your call and obeyed:
Abraham and Sarah, who left the settled land for an unknown journey;
Moses, who risked a desert journey;
Isaiah, who heard your whisper in the temple;
Amos, who trembled at your voice in the market-place;
and Ruth, who crossed the boundaries of a culture.

We are inspired by the trust
of the first disciples by the lakeside,
of Mary, who waited longingly in the garden,
of Paul, blinded by truth on the Damascus road,
and John, exiled on an island.
For these all risked everything for you:
set out on a journey,
the destination veiled from their sight.

We rejoice, gracious God,
that you still call, and people still respond:
followers in the way you intend,
bearers of grace to an often harsh world.
We gather as your people,
ready to hear.
Speak, gracious God.
We are your servants,
and we are listening.

147 Eternal God, Father and Lord,
we are here not alone of our own deciding;
we have heard your compelling voice in so many ways,
and come to you through the witness of so many people:
parents have spoken to their children
and, better, have lived out lives of truth;
friends have shared the good news with friends
and, better, have lived the news in love and care;
the Church has preached its sermons, told its story
and, better, has turned sermons into a community of living faith.

We ask, Lord God,
that as we have heard, so may we speak,
as we have shared, so may we live,
as we have preached, so may we give
and, better, that we may be Christ for others
day by day.

May our worship on this day so prepare us.

148 Eternal God,
you are a God of good news,
always seeking to address your world;
speak to our hearts this day
so that we can share in your communicating.

Open our ears
to hear
what you have to share through Scripture and saint.
Open our hearts
to receive
your call through the cries of the world's wounded.
Open our arms
to embrace
our neighbours in compassion and care.
Open our mouths
to pass on
words and thoughts which glorify you.
Open our minds
to sift and weigh
what we experience and feel.
Open our churches
as communities
where words of hope and love are made flesh.
Open doors of opportunity
so that your voice can be heard
through our sharing and caring;
to the glory of Jesus Christ, our Lord.

149 Gracious God,
we stand amazed that you call us
to speak the truth of the gospel's ways
to the world.

Forgive us that we are sometimes silent:
failing to praise;
shrinking from prayer;
shying from sharing that hope in our hearts.

Forgive us that we listen eagerly for easy truth:
fleeing to gods of worldly persuasion;
falling to the temptation of smooth tongues.

Forgive us that we sing strange songs:
betraying our hearts' true devotion;
revealing our wayward wills.

Forgive us when we turn from and not for faith:
denying your grace;
rejecting your gifts.

Forgive us for the hurt we cause:
words, deeds and thoughts
twisting the knife.

Forgive us for the healing we withhold:
hands not offered in love;
hearts hardened to need.

Forgive us for failing to embody the gospel:
making ourselves no living sacrifice;
making ourselves the centre of our concern.

Forgive us, Lord,
in Jesus' name.

150 We confess our sin, gracious God.
We confess our deliberate frustration of your will for us,
our preference to follow our own will instead.
We confess our deliberate turning from the vision for us you give,
too scared and too selfish to want to serve as you call.
We confess that there are things in our lives of which we are not even aware
that are contrary to the way you want us to be.
Forgive us for the sin of which we are aware,
and the sin so deep we cannot see.
Cleanse us completely, we pray,
that we might love and serve you with faithful hearts and fruitful lives,
and your gospel's good news be known
even through us.

151 Merciful God, accept, we pray, the sorrow we express,
for we know we have failed you.
Thoughts, words and actions of ours
have been against your will.
Inaction, silence and thoughtlessness
have been equally rebellious.
Forgive us our failings.
Heal, we pray, the hurt we have caused,
and breathe new conviction into our discipleship.
For Christ's sake.

152 Patient God,
we are foolish friends of Jesus.
We never seem to learn.
Like Simon Peter of old
we blunder into action
without thought or consideration.

We think that we can save the world.
We imagine that we possess the gospel.
We treat other people as ignorant and benighted.
We are arrogant with the faith you have given us.

Forgive us
  for failing to listen to you;
  for prejudging individuals and situations
    and therefore doing your judging for you;
  for turning good news into bad news
    by increasing the guilt of those to whom we speak.
Forgive us
  for being impatient,
    expecting and seeking instant results;
  for imagining that we are bringing you to people
    when in reality you are there already;
  for not expecting to be changed ourselves
    and to hear you speaking through stranger and sufferer.

Let your forgiveness surround us;
  may our humility increase;
  may we be changed
  into more fitting channels of your good news.

153 Seldom-silent God, we thank you.
Yours was the voice of light in creation's dark,
the voice of order in creation's chaos,
the voice of life in creation's barrenness.

Seldom-silent God, we thank you.
Yours was the voice of a people's calling
through Abraham, and those who came after him.
Yours was the voice of judgement through prophets
when the people lost their way.
Yours was the voice of the psalmists
learning new words of praise.

Seldom-silent God, we thank you.
In Christ, flesh articulated your Word,
and love was expressed for the world.
In Christ, your Word of forgiveness and renewal was focused
in a life spent for our sakes.

Seldom-silent God, we thank you.
Still you speak;
still the gospel's good news transforms lives.
By your Spirit
still people know light and order and life;
still know your calling and judgement;
still know your forgiveness and renewal.

Seldom-silent God, through long years, and in every place
your people have learned to break their own silence
and, by the same Spirit, to tell out the good news
and live out its grace.

Seldom-silent God,
never can we be silent
until your love is known throughout creation.

154 We thank you for the Bible
and its insights into your ways with us,
Gracious God.

We thank you
for its inspiring stories
and its account of humbling failures,
for its chronicle of new hope and restoration,
and its history of the bumbling and stumbling
of your people on the road to truth.

We thank you
for people of faith and courage along the way;
channels of your grace,
inspiring others by speaking your Word
of challenge and change.

Above all, we thank you for Christ
the light for our world,
embodying your initiative of love,
proclaiming your offer of forgiveness,
and calling us to share his cross-bound road.
We pray that we may respond wholeheartedly,
in Christ's name.

155 If only we could leave it in the past, eternal God: this gospel story.
We've read the tale, and marvelled at the courage and conviction.
We've entered the joy, and even felt something of the pain ourselves.
But let it all be past:
a fine example and inspiring story.
Then life would be so much easier for us,
the burden bearable, our time our own.

And yet we cannot.
Your Spirit is present reality, not past example.
Your loving gifts flow now as then.
Still, in the name of Jesus, women and men are guided into truth;
still fractured souls are healed;
still love bursts out afresh;
still faith is born anew,
and still the call resounds to share good news.

Gracious God, we thank you for all that impels us to service:
  your call is whispered in our ears;
  your word sounds out from Bible, pulpit, hymn;
  the human need to hear the word of truth is clear;
  and lives distorted long for healing balm.

We cannot leave it in the past, eternal God: this gospel story.
The tale is true, the courage and conviction real;
the joy not ours to covet for ourselves,
and even something of the pain must be made known.
We pray for wisdom and for strength.
Give us the courage to speak and act in Christ's own name,
confident that your Spirit gives us words to speak.
In Jesus' name we pray.

156

Thank you, God, for your Word:
  made known through prophets;
  made firm through scripture;
  made flesh in Christ;
  made present by your Spirit.
Thank you also, God, that you speak
to us and through us.
Thank you, God, for all who have laboured long and hard
to hear and know, and to show your word for all the world.

Thank you, God, that you are never without witnesses,
that countless quiet and faithful people, listening, wait on you;
ready to hear, willing to speak.
In the clamour of competing voices,
thank you that your Word can still be heard.
Make us expectant to hear, ready to respond
and willing to change.
In Christ's name.

157 Living God,
today our thanks
are for the transparent saints:

humble Christians through whose lives
people can see you without having to try;

writers whose poems, novels or speeches are so inspired
that readers can see your ways and hopes for humanity;

musicians and composers who so lift people's hearts
that they feel they are in heaven itself;

artists who in portraying scenes of pain or joy
give to the world eternal signs of beauty and possibility;

preachers whose passion for proclaiming Jesus
fills their congregations with commitment and new life;

doctors and nurses whose hands and eyes
become practical channels of the Kingdom of God;

teachers whose knowledge and thoughtfulness bring
from their listeners a thirst for deeper meaning in their lives;

politicians and leaders whose courageous decisions
show their citizens your compassionate face;

children whose innocent love of life and freedom from prejudice
show us God-given gifts which many adults have lost;

sufferers whose bearing of pain and serenity in tragedy
make us ashamed of our grumbles,
and who have deepened our faith and hope in you.

Transparent to you,
channels of love,
laying bare the Kingdom,
shining lights in a dark world,
they glorify you and bring from our lips heartfelt praise,
now and always.

158 Bless your Church, here and around the world, Gracious God. May we be led by your Spirit, filled by your grace, committed to your will and devoted to your service. May we find the words to say to all who ask to know the hope we have within us.

Yours is a Spirit of light and life, but too often darkness, despair and death are known. We pray for all who suffer in the present and fear for the future, and find weary troubles weigh so heavy that their eyes never lift to the heavens.

Bless those we know personally who need our love and yours. Give us the grace, we pray, that by word, action and prayer we may be for them the light of love they crave. In Jesus' name.

159 Loving God, whose living Word is active now, sharp as any two-edged sword: we pray for all for whom life is a confusing cacophony of tempting, persuasive and oppressive voices pulling this way and that, and shattering their resolve. We pray that they may hear your voice above the clamour.
We pray for ourselves: that we may learn to 'be still', knowing you are God, waiting on you, listening to you. Imperfect channels though we are, still may your grace, mercy and peace be known through us.
We pray for your Church: that we may be attentive to your voice and courageous to proclaim your word. Deepen our life together as your Church.
We ask our prayers in the name and for the sake of your Word become flesh, Jesus Christ our Lord.

160 Living God,
bless your Church in the world.
May it stand as a sign of hope for all,
and an example of love to the world.
May it be faithfully Christ-like,
responding to its mission,
not counting the cost of commitment,
but paying the price of faith,
and rejoicing in the joy of our common calling
to proclaim the good news of the gospel.

We pray for those given tasks that aid our mission:
leaders within our churches;
staffs of colleges;
directors of training;
youth leaders and children's work officers;
and all whose calling is to enable the whole body of Christ
to be the Church of your will for the world;
making the good news known, and your love shown.

161

How many people Jesus met!
He loved them all.
He healed the sick.
He told them of God's love and care.
Good news for all the people Jesus met.

How many people we all meet!
Help us, Lord, to love.
Help us to be true friends.
Help us to share our love for God.
Good news for all the people we meet.

162

Help us, Father God,
to put the gospel into action
and preach it with our lives.

Help us to welcome strangers and newcomers,
and make people feel wanted and cared for.
Help us to listen to the ideas of other people,
and take their opinions seriously.
Help us to notice when people are sad,
and be sensitive to their needs.
Help us to be alert to the lonely,
and offer Christian friendship.
Help us to hear the cry of anguish or pain,
and stand alongside those who need us.
We dare to ask that we may grow more like Christ himself,
and so help others to find his love.

163 Living God,
how beautiful are the feet
of those who carry
the gospel of peace;
how great is the company
of the preachers,
whose voice goes out into all the world.
Support, we pray,
these your servants.

Living God,
how blessed are the merciful,
the mourners,
the meek
and the peacemakers,
who are your words made flesh in the world.
Strengthen, we pray,
these your servants.

Living God,
how wonderful
are those communities of faith
who act with courage and conviction
to address their neighbourhoods,
who face opposition from alternative propaganda,
and who are agents of reconciliation and peace.
Come close, we pray,
to these your servants.

Living God,
how humbling it is
to hear of Christians
who are imprisoned and tortured
because they have dared to speak out in your name
against tyrannical governments and oppressive leaders.
They are your prophets and saints of our generation.
Encourage, we pray,
these your servants,
and every quiet saint
whose life speaks out today
in the spirit of Jesus Christ,
our Risen Lord.

164 Living God,
seen in the face of Christ,
and known in the power and presence of your Spirit,
we rejoice that your Word is vibrant;
still surprising, still upsetting,
still sweet to taste, still transforming lives.
Your Word turns tables;
heals broken hearts; confronts injustice;
breathes life; brings hope;
shares pain; speaks love;
became flesh in Christ,
and becomes known by your Spirit.
By our words and deeds may we bear your Word in our lives.

165 Almighty God,
who called Abraham to leave his land,
  we too hear your call to sacrifice.
Gathering God,
who led your people from slavery to freedom,
  we too hear your call to follow.
Loving God,
who walked a royal road to wood and nails,
  we too hear your call to deny ourselves.
Inspiring God,
who came like flame-tongues on pilgrims,
  we too hear your call to set minds alight
    with the good news of the gospel.
'Here we are, Lord, send us!'

166 Loving God,
Jesus, your Son, lived our life:
knew our highs and our lows,
our happy and our sad;
called the Church to be,
and sent it into the world
on a mission to make your love known,
and your will shown.
We pray that we may faithfully play our part
in your continuing mission.
In Jesus' name.

167 We remember, calling God,
that you loved the world so much
that you sent your Son;
we remember that Jesus loved so much
that he was willing to die on the cross;
we remember that Jesus' disciples
were marked out by their love for each believer,
and for others.
We pray that we may live up to our calling.
For the sake of Jesus Christ our Lord.

168 Calling God,
your voice was known in Creation,
speaking light and life into darkness and emptiness.
Your voice was known in a people,
calling them to be light in the darkness of idolatry.
Your voice was known in the person of Jesus,
challenging followers to bring life to the world,
and filling emptiness with purpose.
Your voice still sounds:
calling people to bear light to the world.
We give thanks for those who hear and respond,
and give of themselves in the service of your Kingdom.
Many are the tasks, calling God,
varied the gifts, and endless the callings.
We commit ourselves to you,
that your Kingdom may come and your will be done.

169 Hands can fight, and push and shove,
Hands can greet, and hold and love,
Father God, for Jesus' sake, may our hands do your work.

Voices can shout, and scream, and bellow,
Voices in welcome can say, 'Hello!',
Father God, for Jesus' sake, may our voices do your work.

People can scorn, get cross, offend,
People can welcome, and find a new friend,
Father God, for Jesus' sake, may we be your people.

170 Lord,
we need a new spirit and a new confidence
as we seek to be your voice
in the communities where we live and work.

Help us to understand
that everything does not depend on us.

Kindle within us a realization
that we are first of all receivers;
empty vessels needing to be filled with your love.

Remind us that we are like clay,
pliable and flexible;
ready to be re-worked and re-formed by you.

Show us how words are not always needed,
but that lives of forgiveness and beauty
are more powerful than words.

When the mouths of the world scream loudly,
reassure us of the victories of small voices.
When the demand is for sensational actions,
take us by the hand
and lead us down the long, patient road
of self-giving and struggle.

When we are overcome by worries
about the future of the Church,
open our eyes to see you working
through a myriad of ways in the world.
When we lose our enthusiasm,
fan the flames of our spirits,
so that we burn with a desire
to announce your goodness and worth.

Let your gospel
be a lamp to our feet
and a light to our path,
inspiring
our words and deeds
to glorify your name.

171 Jesus,
through your roots in a Jewish home,
remind us
of all we owe to our families and friends,
and all we have gained from our culture and environment.

Through your discoveries of faith
in synagogue and scripture,
show us
how important it is
to know God as our father and friend.

Through your questioning and wondering
as a bar-mitzvah boy,
give us an appetite
for searching and enquiry
so that our minds are open
and our hearts tolerant
in the quest for truth.

Led by you
to thankfulness,
life and truth
as children of God,
let our lives
resound with new songs
and our lives ring with joy,
for you are indeed
Immanuel,
God-with-us,
yesterday, today and for ever.

172 Lord Jesus Christ,
we pray that we
who are amongst those
who most frequently mention your name
may also be found amongst those
who most urgently seek your truth,
most deeply explore your ways
and most readily live in your resurrection light.

173 Risen Christ,
as ice melts and rivers flow
when spring comes,
breathe your life-giving Spirit
into our frozen hearts.
Set our minds on fire,
and our feet running,
to seek and serve your truth.
Free us from all that captivates us.
Give us a deeper understanding of your truth.
Increase our wisdom.
Remind us that you have written our names
on the palms of your crucified hands,
and help us to know that you call us by name.

174 Too many words
spoken without thought
fill our lives, Jesus,
when a silent deed
in your name
would be a million times
more effective,
and the world
would know that God
is most vocal
in becoming flesh,
    and is seen
    and touched
    and known.

If we become
hollow vessels;
wordy, boring and hypocritical,
silence our tiresome tongues
and let us speak only when we have
praise to offer you,
in response
to your mighty deeds
in human lives.

175 Lord, a blind and blinkered world
cries out for help.
Son of David: **Have mercy on us.**

Lord, you have spoken to us
through prophet and poet,
author and playwright,
but we have closed our ears.
Son of David: **Have mercy on us.**

Lord, you have shown us what we must do to worship you in truth:
to do justly; to love mercy;
to walk humbly with you;
but we have shut our eyes.
Son of David: **Have mercy on us.**

Lord, you have walked with us in Jesus Christ
and loved alongside us;
then in painful love
you displayed your purpose
for the world;
but we rejected your presence.
Son of David: **Have mercy on us.**

Lord, teach us and heal us;
break open our ears;
restore to us our sight,
so that in sudden clarity
we can see the way we ought to go.
Then we can search diligently for your peace,
work tirelessly for your justice
and offer a humble worship
which honours your name.

176 Father,
we do not find it easy
to retain our enthusiasm
for growing and learning,
for searching and discovering.
Rekindle our desire to seek your truth.

Father,
we do not find it easy
to listen for wisdom
in other cultures and traditions,
in the words of playwright and poet,
in children's dreams,
or old folk's memories.
  Open our minds to receive your truth.

177 Father, our world is crying out for wise thoughts:
  thoughts which are unselfish and genuine;
  thoughts which search for your truth
    in our human situation.
Forgive us:
  for muddled minds which result in stupid decisions;
  for superficial thinking which skates past life and death.
Let your wisdom possess our thoughts, leading us to the mind of Christ.

Father, our world is crying out for wise words:
  words which are commitments in themselves;
  words which are filled with integrity and hope.
Forgive us:
  for foolish talk of peace when there is no peace;
  for silly words of bravado
    designed to cover confusion or ignorance;
  for shallow promises
    which pay lip-service to the needs of others.
Let your wisdom penetrate our conversation,
  filling it with the words of Christ.

Father, our world is crying out for wise actions:
  actions which go the extra mile of sacrificial care;
  actions which reconcile and unite the human family.
Forgive us:
  for deeds half-complete
    leaving people anxious and frustrated;
  for frantic energy
    which never gets to the heart of people's pain.
Let your wisdom permeate our actions,
enabling us to share the ministry of Christ.

178 Precious
beyond jewels
is the treasure of your Word,
living God.

Precious
are the words of psalmists and prophets:
  reflecting the pain of national crisis and personal tragedy;
  announcing their thankfulness for the way
    your powerful hand has rescued
    and restored.

Precious
are the counsels of wise thinkers:
  searching for answers to eternal questions;
  probing the mysteries of the universe;
  pondering the reason for good and evil,
    success and failure,
    joy and suffering.

Precious
is the unfolding story of your journey with your people:
  a story of promise and fulfilment,
    exile and restoration,
    judgement and forgiveness.

Precious
is the gospel of Jesus,
  for he is good news to the poor,
    healing to the broken,
    and peace to a dislocated world.

Precious
also
are the words you give each of us to say
today
and always.

179 Risen Jesus,
where else can we go?
You have the words of eternal life.

We have listened to the sound of politicians
and the arguments of philosophers;
we have been coaxed by the media
and exhorted by the press;
we have heard the doom and destruction preachers
who urge us to flee the world;
but where shall we go?
You have the words of eternal life.

Thank you, Lord,
for coming to us
where we are,
not to pluck us away
to some heavenly kingdom,
but to send us back
into the city,
into the noise,
into the world
of half-baked answers and selfish ideologies.

Thank you for promising to feed us
with the bread of your presence
wherever we travel.
And when our bodies are tired,
and our hearts are broken
by the pain of the world,
we know you are especially close.

Come near, Lord,
so that we may know ourselves
to be your body,
shared and broken
in love for your world.

180 O God,
patient and forgiving,
reaching out to us in eternal welcome,
carrying us in tender understanding,
you have always declared your way for the world
through the graciousness of your character
and the teaching of Jesus.

When people try to convince us
that it is foolish and unrealistic
to forgive and forget:
help us to learn the lessons of history;
to call on our own experiences;
to remember the teaching of Jesus
and to set the cross central to our lives.

When people try to persuade us
that it is weakness and folly
to take second place and make room for others:
help us to learn the lessons of history;
to call on our own experiences;
to remember the teaching of Jesus
and to set the cross central to our lives.

When people try to prove to us
that this life is all that matters,
and death is final:
help us to learn the lessons of history;
to call on our own experiences;
to remember the teaching of Jesus
and to set the cross central to our lives,
that we who need to learn so much
may be teachers of a weary and disillusioned world.

181 Lord, let silence speak and teach its own truth:
let the sleeping child speak of vulnerability;
let the silent dawn speak of hope;
let the urgency of spring speak of growth;
let the single rose in its vase speak of earth's beauty
and let silent prayer be eloquent praise.

182 As a shepherd
seeks the lost sheep;
as a woman searches for the lost coin;
Parent God, seek and search for us,
for we have wandered far from home.
We have lost touch
with what nourishes and stretches us.
We have missed the mark,
aiming at false security
instead of seeking the goal of the Kingdom.
We have preferred prosperity
to the cutting edge of life lived in your presence.
We have bowed down to the idol of expediency
and neglected to tend the gifts of the Spirit.

Christ, who makes whole,
bring us back from the precipice.
Holy Spirit, who leads us into all truth,
bring us home to God.

183 *Whoever hears these words of mine and acts on them is like a man who had the sense to build his house on rock.* *Matthew 7. 24*

O Creator of the earth,
save us from the insecurity of sand;
sinking, shifting, sliding.

O Saviour of the world,
help us to build on rock;
stable, safe, sure.

O Renewer of life,
bring us to the promised land;
changed, reformed, rebuilt.

184

Lord,
we keep listening
for your voice
in the wrong places.
We forget that your word
is at its most powerful
when it seems weakest.

We forget that Elijah
was a lonely voice
in a noisy Israel.

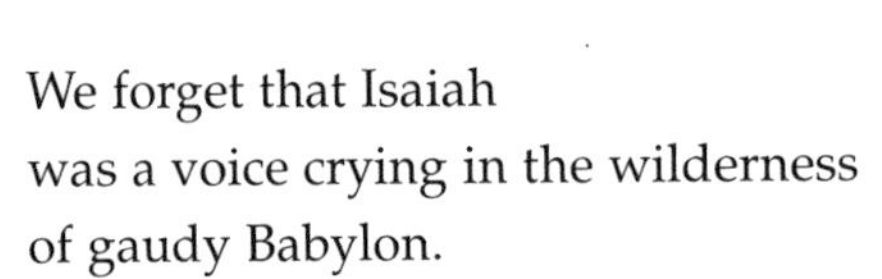

We forget that Isaiah
was a voice crying in the wilderness
of gaudy Babylon.

We forget that Jesus'
dying words
floated almost unnoticed
over festive Jerusalem.

Help us to listen more closely
to the lonely prophets of today:
to black poets in a white culture;
to minority leaders
speaking for forgotten groups of people;
to ghetto voices who grieve for friends
left behind in a nation's race for wealth;
to unpopular preachers
who question the integrity of governments;
to journalists and politicians
who work tirelessly to uncover truth.

And may your lonely word
be on our lips too
when you have a message
to proclaim to your people.

185 Thank you, Father,
for the timeless words
of the gospel writers
with their differing perspectives
on Jesus' teaching.

To all entrusted with teaching,
our prayers reach out today:
that they may engage fearlessly in the search for wisdom;
that they may have skill in communication;
and a genuine love for the minds and lives
of all whom they teach.

As seeds of hope are sown
in schools, churches and places of further education
by people who have glimpsed your Kingdom,
may people of all nations
see what no mortal eye sees
and hear what no mortal ear hears
and reach towards
things at present beyond their mental horizon,
but in range of your loving purpose.

186 Lord God, give us your strength,
that we may live courageously as friends of Jesus.
Surround our lives with your truth:
a truth which penetrates false motives;
a truth which uncovers corruption and hypocrisy;
a truth arrived at by patient searching and honest questioning.
Speak to us your word through the Spirit:
a word revealing your deeper purposes;
a word earthed in Jesus our Lord;
a word given to us when we do not know what to say.
And thus made strong,
may we live out the truth day by day,
and proclaim the word with integrity and hope.

187 Lord Jesus, your teaching
was given in the language of the people;
used examples that sprang from their daily life;
did no disservice to their own experience of life;
and valued the intelligence and thoughtfulness of those who heard you.
Help us in the task you have given us of sharing your message with others.
When we teach children
help us to value the experience of life they have already enjoyed;
When we teach young people
help us to be sensitive in their time of growth and rebellion;
When we teach older people
help us to listen for insights we have not ourselves experienced;
When we teach strangers and newcomers
help us to remember that you have walked alongside them through their years;
When we teach those from cultures other than our own
help us to recognize that you are present in every life-style;
Whoever we teach,
help us to be learners, in Jesus' name.

188 Lord,
I know your commandments off by heart
but that is only the beginning.
Your Kingdom is beyond the recitation of the familiar.
Write your law of love
not upon my memory only,
but upon my heart
so that it is strained and tested
daily.

189 When the prophets of doom
proclaim the end of the world,
and the majority of people
live only for the pleasures of the present,
give us a different outlook.
Help us to hold fast to a realistic belief
in your creative power;
a power which has not burnt itself out
but which can be experienced first-hand
by all who truly seek you.

May we take up your journey in good heart,
seeking a more mature grasp of your goal
for all creation
until we indeed discover
your glorious fullness
in Jesus Christ, our Lord.

190 Jesus, teacher,
do I hear you clearly?
I come to you
expecting a lecture, a programme,
a list of dos and don'ts.
But here you are
inviting me to walk with you
and learn as I go.

Who will speak, Lord?
Will it be the leper and the prisoner?
Will it be the widow and the orphan?
Will it be the foreigner and the traveller?
Will it be the prostitute and the thief?

Will it be the debt-ridden countries of Africa?
Will it be the young man sleeping beneath a cardboard box?
Will it be the child abused, the woman threatened?
Will it be the woman who works from home for a pittance?
Will it be the political exile knocking on Britain's door?

Jesus, Lord and God,
as I walk with you
and listen,
keep me alert
wherever you speak.

191 God of stillness,
hold us in your presence
that, taking your stillness into ourselves,
we may be truly present to others.

God of care-fulness,
hold us in your love
that, taking your caring into ourselves,
we may be genuinely loving towards others.

God of attentiveness,
hold us within your gentle power to wait
that, taking your attention into ourselves,
we may wait for, and wait upon, others.

192 When nothing is right,
when we are weary and lost,
when clouds dull the sky,
help us to be still.

When our cries are unheeded,
when no effort bears fruit,
when the sun sets,
help us to be still.

When love is over,
when hope is gone,
when darkness covers the land,
help us to be still.

For in being still,
in refusing to panic or despair,
we shall come to know
that God is there,
suffering alongside and with us,
waiting to show us stepping-stones
through the swirling waters,
and to help us
sing a new song.

193

As the grey wave
creeps on to the shore
and the sail limps
for port,
so, Lord, do I
throw myself
into your harbour; crawl into the circle
of your welcoming arms.

May I know your forgiveness.
Then may I forgive
as you have forgiven me.

And now the blue comes flooding in,
transforming sea and sky with light;
the white wave tops are bracelets of glory;
the sand
a new page
on which to write my story.

194

Make time to sit in comfort,
to breathe deeply,
to relax in the presence of God,
like a cat asleep on a chair
or a rabbit sunnily on a path.

The Loving One, who made you,
who yearned over you in the womb,
who cherished you as a baby,
who tended you as a child,
who gave you glimpses of glory
from your pram;
the One who moulded you,
the One whose loving arm is always
under your head,
says:
'Have no fear for I have redeemed you.
I call you by name and you are mine'.

I, ... , am loved by God.
Keep silence in that thought.

195 Sometimes
I long to call
words of praise
to me,
so that they may settle
like doves on my palm.
I long to coax them
down from the trees
into my waiting hands.

Sometimes they come,
swift and powerful,
like hawks to the wrist of the falconer;
words of challenge,
fierce words of regret.

One time you came:
The Word;
not at my call.
    You came
    to occupy
    a cradle, a grave,
    my heart,
    the universe.
    You came to call me to unleash
    words of comfort,
    words of hope.

Sometimes
I hold out
my empty hands,
and wait.

196 Breathe in time with the rhythm of the earth:
ebbing tide, night and day; seasons of rest, growth, beauty and fruitfulness.
Breathe in time with your own being:
beat of heart, rate of pulse, patterns of work and rest.
Breathe in time with the Spirit of God:
breadth of prayer, depth of solitude, height of hopefulness.
Breathe in time with silence; be still and know that he is God.

197 I stand.
I open myself to God.
I kneel.
I listen.
I step into God's presence.
I float in the encompassing ocean of God's love.
I breathe in and out:
breathing in the mercy of God,
breathing out the pain of my sadness.

I am still,
at rest with God
who is deep within me,
and all around me.

Out of that deep centre
I weave a prayer
of God's presence,
affirming that God is:
that God is with the poor;
that God is with the outcast;
that God is with me.

I call upon God's Spirit.
She rests like a butterfly
shimmering on a branch.
She confronts the hurt
which lies twisted
in the heart of society.

She leads me out
from active prayer
into prayerful action.

Creating, sustaining and all-loving God,
give us the strength and courage to be still,
that we might better serve your broken world.

198 Let silence be placed around us
like a mantle.
Let us enter into it,
as through a small, secret door;
stooping,
to emerge into
an acre of peace
where stillness reigns,
and God is ever present.

Silence

Then comes the voice of God,
in the startled cry
of a refugee child,
waking
in unfamiliar surroundings.

Then comes the voice of God,
in the mother,
fleeing with
her treasure
in her arms and saying:
'I am here'.

Then comes the voice of God,
in the father
who points to the stars
and says:
'There is our signpost;
there is our lantern.
Be of good courage.'

Silence

O Lord, may the mantle of silence
become a cloak of understanding
to warm our hearts in prayer.

199 Gracious God,
light of hope in the darkness of confusion,
depth of love seen in the death of your Son,
we give thanks for the silence of faith and trust
at the heart of our calling:
a silence of 'letting go';
of 'being still' to hear again;
and know and build our lives on the truth of the gospel.

We give thanks
for the beauty and power and healing of silence –
the haven of stillness in a world of noise.
But we especially give thanks
for the silence which becomes
your creative Word.

The following prayers have been written for use during a Quiet Day.

200 *At the beginning:* Mysterious God,
we seek a safe place, a listening-place,
in which to open ourselves
and be available – and vulnerable –
to the still, small voice.

201 *Part-way through:* Strengthening God,
thank you for filling our empty hands
with the bread of quietness,
and our dry hearts
with the waters of your compassion.

202 *At the end:* Sending God,
now that we find the listening-place within ourselves,
and are nourished with stillness,
we are ready to walk the risk-filled roads,
and hold out your gift of quiet to other pilgrims.

203 Living God,
your voice is not silent,
your hands are not withdrawn;
you still address the nations
and you still reach out to them in welcome.

As we worship you this day,
fill us with a strong sense of your universal presence.
You are closer to us than our life-breath
and yet you are also the righteous God of all creation.

Like the warm sun on our faces
or the spring breeze in our hair
you touch our lives each day.
Yet you are equally concerned with governments
and with empires and with industrial giants.

Help us to see you, not as a private mascot,
but in all your glory,
so that we are moved as you are with deep compassion;
angered as you are with human arrogance;
active as you are in peace and reconciliation;
close as you are to the victims of injustice.

Then we can dare to be called
the people of Jesus Christ, our Lord.

204 All-seeing God,
We confess to you
That although we long for justice for ourselves
We are slow to seek justice for others,
Especially if it costs us dear.
And we confess to you
That, although we pray for peace for our world,
We find it hard to keep the peace ourselves,
With our family, our friends, within our church.

Saving God,
You alone can break down the barriers
    that divide us one from another;
    that we build between us and you;
    that keep us from your perfect Kingdom
    of justice, peace and love.
We ask your forgiveness for all our sins
Against humanity and against you,
In the name of Jesus Christ, our Saviour,
Who died to make us one.

205 Scarred,
battered,
bleeding is your world,
crucified God.

Weeping,
grieving,
hungry are your children,
Mother God.

Blind,
hard,
proud are the nations,
mighty God.

Helpless,
confused,
weak is your Church,
forgiving God.

Take from us the guilt of our failures, gracious God,
but do not take away the pain
until we are stirred to do all in our power
and yours
so that peace and hope and love are not distant dreams
but present experiences for all your children,
through Jesus Christ.

206 Lord, we thank you
For all those whom your Spirit has inspired
To work for justice and peace:
For the prophets, who proclaim your word,
challenging people to live justly,
encouraging them to seek true, lasting peace;
For organizations who work for world harmony,
who try to open the eyes of leaders
to the wisdom of just government
and the folly of war;
For individuals who risk themselves and their freedom
in their struggles to see justice established,
in their efforts to make peace.
Lord, we thank you
For all who strive for justice and peace
And for sending us your Son, Jesus Christ
to show us the true justice
that meets our deepest needs;
to show us the true peace
that transfigures human lives;
to show us your perfecting love
that breaks down all barriers
and redeems the world.

207 Spirit of God,
like the wind
you still move over the waters of chaos,
bringing order from confusion,
sweeping away the old and bringing in the new.

We rejoice in your transforming power.

Spirit of God,
like fire
you still judge the hearts of evil leaders,
uncovering their deeds of violence,
displaying the folly of war and bloodshed.

We rejoice in your righteous power.

Spirit of God,
like a dove
you still descend upon a divided world,
softening the hearts of the intransigent,
drawing enemies to the table of peace.

We rejoice in your reconciling power.

Spirit of God,
like a wise counsellor
you still sow seeds of truth in the hearts of humanity,
helping those who decide to see new perspectives,
challenging the assumptions of the lazy and prejudiced.

We rejoice in your mind-changing power.

Spirit of God,
like breath
you still give life to communities which are facing death,
raising up prophets to speak fearlessly,
empowering your Church to bring hope and renewal.

We rejoice in your resurrection power.

Spirit of God,
like a comforting mother
you still dry the tears of those who have been wronged,
raising the wounded to their feet
and giving them the courage to sing new songs.

We rejoice in your gentle power.

Spirit of God,
like fragrance
you pervade all of existence,
reconciling, peace-making, loving, renewing.

We rejoice in your powerful presence.

208 Loving King,
There is so much injustice in your world:
Injustice in families,
  where not all are given the same rights or respect;
Injustice in countries,
  where some are oppressed, exploited, discriminated against,
  while others wallow in power or wealth;
Injustice between nations,
  where some are destitute, hungry, in debt,
  so that others can live too well.

Lord, we pray for all those who are the victims of injustice of any kind,
  and especially for ...
  Lord, in your mercy: **Hear our prayer.**

Loving King,
There is so much conflict in your world:
Conflict in families,
  leading to deep wounds and unhappiness;
Conflict in countries,
  between races, classes, religions,
  leading to suspicion, violence and fear;
Conflict between nations,
  broken relations, skirmishes, wars,
  leading to great suffering and pain.

Lord, we pray for all those who are the victims of conflict of any kind,
  and especially for ...
  Lord, in your mercy: **Hear our prayer.**

Loving King,
we pray for justice, peace and reconciliation in our relationships,
in our society and in our world.
We pray for the coming of your Kingdom.
In Jesus the Saviour's name.

209 God of nations
new and old,
near at hand
or far away,
touch with your presence
the tense and crucial situations
where those with power are under stress
and those without it are finding a voice.
Let there be an atmosphere of growing trust,
a willingness to listen
and a reliance upon dialogue rather than threat
among negotiators and politicians.

Open eyes
which have been closed
by centuries of bigotry and dogmatism;
soften hearts
which have been hardened by fear;
release wisdom from minds
which have been dulled by mistrust.

Then let the continents sing of justice without revenge
and the emerging nations speak of freedom without recrimination;
may cynical minds discover hope,
idle hands be moved to action,
and hearts of dread warm to deeds of compassion.

For you still create new heavens and a new earth
before our eyes
through the power of your son, Jesus Christ.

210 Lord, we know that we are infinitely precious to you,
That you love each of us like a daughter or son,
That you have no favourites,
And long for justice for all your children.
Lord, with the help of your Spirit,
We will strive for the justice you long for,
We will seek the coming of your Kingdom.

Lord, you fill our lives with lasting peace;
Not the easy peace of apathy or indifference
But the peace that comes from knowing your love
And learning to love you, others and ourselves.
Lord, with the help of your Spirit,
We will strive to let your peace grow,
We will seek the coming of your Kingdom.

Lord, teach us the art of true loving,
That the world may know itself truly loved by you.
Make us one, that the world might believe,
And be reconciled in you.

211

Holy God,
our ears are ringing with the sounds of voices
crying out in distress:
people without names yet whose faces stare at us each day;
children malnourished, mothers beyond hope in their grief;
fathers helpless to provide, devastated by famine and trapped by war.

So we too cry out in despair.
We cry to you,
the God of babies and mothers and fathers.
We cry to you for justice
and for help to know what on earth to do.

When our ears are deaf because the cries are too familiar,
help us to respond with urgency once more.
When our tears have dried up because we have seen it all before,
rekindle our sympathy and our generosity.
When our anger has abated because cruelty is a fact of life,
stir within us a new sense of justice.

Save us from hypocrisy:
speaking words of peace but not making peace;
praying for reconciliation but not daring to build bridges;
criticizing politicians but remaining hard-hearted at home.

Save us from apathy:
leaving the hard work to others;
complaining that we can't do anything about injustice;
failing to get involved in issues in our local community.

Save us from insensitivity:
going along with the selfishness of society;
reinforcing the prejudices of our culture;
failing to notice the needs on our doorsteps.

Save us from a comfortable gospel:
designed to save our own souls only;
aimed at the Church rather than the world;
expecting the glory without the pain,
the resurrection without the cross.

Save us from making Jesus into a harmless mascot:
a comforter but not a challenger;
a story-teller but not a debater;
a donkey-rider but not a turner-over of tables;
a teacher but not a transformer;
a lover but not a redeemer.

Then may we be better equipped
to be people of your Kingdom
which confronts and challenges
the division and hatred in the world,
to the glory of your holy name.

212

God of justice, encircle the earth
and let the nations live in harmony;
Prince of peace, heal your divided world
and let the nations live in harmony;
Spirit of reconciliation, breathe your gentleness on all creation
and let the nations live in harmony;
Holy Trinity,
let justice, peace and reconciliation prevail
and the nations live in harmony.

213 Loving God, we come to you
Wearied and appalled by the evil of our world.
We long to turn our tear-filled eyes
From the sights of injustice, oppression,
and the sufferings of its victims,
And rest them upon you, our Just Judge,
And praise you for the beauty of your justice.
We long to stop listening, for a while,
To the horrific sounds of warfare,
and the cries of the wounded and lost,
To hear again sweet words of peace and comfort,
And praise you for your victory over sin.

Loving God, we come to you,
Bringing with us a world torn apart
By cruelty, selfishness and hatred,
To pray for the strength to strive for your Kingdom;
To pray that in your love all might be made one.
In the name of Love Victorious: Jesus Christ, our Lord.

214 A Meditation: Reconciliation as God's Gift

We face each other
across a raw divide.
The chasm of our anger
filled with the bones
of old hatreds.

The wounded earth
spews out our greed
in acrid smoke.
The gaping world cries out in pain.

The upward surge of birds in flight,
wheeling and dancing
in the sun,
the sound of geese
strung across an empty sky,
the scent of blossom on the wind;
are gifts of a generous Creator,
to lift, to call, to heal.

215 Jesus, full of compassion,
our strength and support,
lover and carer of bodies and souls,
we come to worship you.

We come to you weakened by our lack of faith;
we come to you wearied by the demands of life;
we come to you wondering about the future.

May our worship be worthy of your unending love,
given freely to help us to get the best from life.
Then send us out into the community
to give our love and support to all in need.

216 *Jesus poured water into a basin, and began to wash his disciples' feet.*

John 13.5

Come, Lord, and bathe our feet,
for we are tired from our journey through life.

Come, Lord, and wash our hands,
for our selfish acts have made us dirty.

Come, Lord, and cleanse our wounds,
for we have been hurt by life's sharp corners.

Then, when we are clean and refreshed, Lord,
travel with us so that we may
bathe the feet of the world's weariness
wash away the selfishness of humanity's self-concern
and cleanse the wounds of human hurt,
for Christ's sake.

217 We look and stare, but what do we see?
A man lame from injury,
a woman with blistered skin,
a boy with eyes that do not respond,
a girl whose face twitches uncontrollably,
that is what we see, all we see.
We do not know, or understand, or look beyond.

God, who loves all equally,
help us to look, and see, and love,
not the obvious surface view
but the real person underneath.

We see and judge, but what do we think?
A man so nervous that he stammers,
a woman whose body is lifeless,
a boy whose emotions are overwhelming,
a girl whose deformity makes her shy,
that is what we see, we judge without thinking.
We do not know, or understand, or look beyond.

God, who knows us through and through,
help us, having seen,
not to be hasty or shallow in our judgements,
but to seek the potential in all people.

All-loving God, you know us and all our faults.
Forgive us when we do not love
as deeply as we should,
as you love us.

218 It is so easy, Lord, to pass by on the other side.
When we see young people hanging around outside the church,
we are more worried about our cars and church windows
than we are about them or the reasons that turn them into vandals.

When we are stopped in the street by a beggar,
we resist the request for spare change
or offer money to avoid questioning a society that produces them.

When we see pictures on the television
of people's lives destroyed by war or natural disaster,
we feel a moment's compassion and then switch programmes
to avoid the tension of judging between aggressor and victim.

In forgiving us, Lord,
show us how to be servants in immediate help,
to be prophets in understanding the cause of human problems
and to be active in creating the world you first intended.

219

Thank you, God:
your thoughts are wiser than our thoughts,
your wisdom greater than our wisdom,
your understanding deeper than our understanding,
your compassion stronger than our compassion.

We thank you that from the beginning of the world you have watched over and cared for each and every person, without prejudice to race, ability, health or achievement.

We thank you for sending Jesus, the person of perfection, who revealed your love in his healing, forgiving, encouraging, challenging ways.

We thank you for filling us with your Spirit of life and love, which enables each of us to know you and love you and speak with you in prayer.

Thank you, God, for all that you have done for us, even when we have not known or appreciated your activity on our behalf. May we show our gratitude to you not only in our words but also in our deeds, so that what we have received may be shared with all whom you love.

220

Lord, we see you at work in the world and come to give you thanks.

When the hungry are fed and the needy clothed,
We thank you because we see your love at work.

When prisoners and patients are visited,
We thank you because we see your love at work.

When the stranger is made at home,
We thank you because we see your love at work.

When people with no power and no voice are listened to with respect,
We thank you because we see your love at work.

When other people care about us and for us,
We thank you because we see your love at work.

When you give us a new chance and a new hope,
We thank you because we see your love at work.

221 Living God, you hold all peoples within your loving care:
no colour, race or gender curbs your graciousness;
time does not weary your love;
there are no barriers, no boundaries to your kindness;
and so we come with gratitude and thankfulness for your universal gifts.

Though, even as we speak with thanksgiving,
a shadow falls across our gratitude.

We hardly dare to thank you that we are free to worship you in peace,
for even as we pray
others worship you in danger,
or under the watchful eye of oppression;
others must measure each word they speak,
lest carelessness invites persecution;
and others whisper their adoration in prison, or in hiding.

We hardly dare to thank you for our health and well-being,
for even as we pray
children are dying for reasons which money could cure;
young men and women live as though already old;
families watch anxiously as loved ones suffer;
and agencies for health are swamped by pleas they cannot meet.

We hardly dare to thank you for the food we eat this day,
for even as we pray
babies cry out in hunger;
little children scavenge the gutters to survive;
and people dream of food they will never see.

We hardly dare to thank you for secure and loving homes,
for even as we pray
families are hounded from place to place;
a father builds a shelter in the sand, close pressed against a neighbour's patch of land;
the dispossessed straggle the countryside to find a homeland;
and youngsters argue as they choose in which doorway they can sleep.

We hardly dare to thank you for our family love,
for even as we pray
an argument disturbs the peace of home;
a father leaves his house to search for work;
a child sits fearful of anger that will strike again;
and parents worry for a son they never see.

Yet thank you now we will, and must,
and to our thanks add holy rage,
and to our rage add promised help,
and to our help, the hope and trust
that justice may be born anew,
and earth become a lovelier place.

222 When did we see you in prison, Lord?
Shut in not by four walls,
  but by an unresponding body:
  limbs which are uncontrolled;
  eyes which are blurred or blind;
  ears which are silent,
    or so filled with noise that it shuts out the right sounds;
  muscles wasted, nerves unfeeling.

When did we see you hungry, Lord?
Yearning not for food but for love:
  a body needing tender comfort;
  inflamed wounds needing soothing,
  diseased and crying out for new drugs,
  a mind tormented by past remembrances
    yet unable to remember a minute ago;
  pain raging, activity frustrated.

When did we see you naked, Lord?
Vulnerable, not without clothes,
  but stripped of dignity and respect:
  unable to restrain bodily functions;
  too weak to complain or fight on;
  unable to form words and communicate
    so that your opinion is not noticed;
  spiritually unfulfilled, humanly disregarded.

Lord, when we see you like this, in our neighbours,
fill us with your compassionate love.

223 You have loved us;
help us to love others.
You have healed us, made us whole, holy;
help us to heal others by helping them to be whole.
You have strengthened us;
so may we strengthen others.
You have shown us compassion;
may we become compassionate.
You carry us through the worst moments;
may we be enabled to carry all who are weak.

God, who loved us first,
fill us with your love
so that all our words and actions
may reveal your divine love in the world.

224 I am weak; give me strength to support the weaknesses in others.
I am sick; make me well enough to tend the sickness in others.
I am limited; make me whole so that I can bring others to wholeness.
I am unworthy of your love; make me open to receive from you
so that I can be open to give to others.
Lord, just as I am, I commit myself to you.
Knowing your commitment to me
assures me that you will help me
in supporting and loving others
by the power of the Holy Spirit.

225 May our church exist for others as it does for ourselves.
May we work as hard for others as we do for ourselves.

May we care as much about others as we do about ourselves.
May we use our gifts as creatively for others as we do for ourselves.

Take the life of our church, our work, our care and our gifts
and use us to serve others in your name.

226 Parent God,
like a mother hen you gather us under your protecting wing;
like a nurse you bind our wounds and tenderly restore our health;
like a father you guide our footsteps along safe paths;
show us through your Son the way that we should speak and act in love to others.

227 Lord, when I see only blindness,
help me to see the person
and the clear-sighted vision within.
When I sense only disablement,
help me to see the person
and the leaping faith and joy within.
When I hear only deafness,
help me to see the person
and the laughter and tears within.
And when I see myself,
help me to see my true self
often blind to truth, crippled in spirit,
and deaf to the prayers of others.

228 I confess it, Lord:
I often give in order to get back in return;
I like to be thought of as generous, even when I'm not;
I sometimes give to impress rather than to please.
To be honest, Lord,
I suspect it will always be the same:
my motives are rarely pure;
my intentions seldom single-minded.
So it's up to you as well as me, Lord:
help me to be more like those who give from true generosity;
help me to serve for the sake of those who need my help;
help me to give and not to count the cost;
help me to spend myself
which I guess, Lord, means, help me to be more like Jesus;
and that's a costly prayer.
And I'm glad that sometimes, just sometimes,
I mean it.

The World Around Us

If you faithfully obey the Lord your God by diligently observing all his commandments which I lay on you this day, then the Lord your God will raise you high above all nations of the earth, and the following blessings will all come and light on you, because you obey the Lord your God.
A blessing on you in the town; a blessing on you in the country.
A blessing on the fruit of your body, the fruit of your land and cattle, the offspring of your herds and lambing flocks.
A blessing on your basket and your kneading trough.
A blessing on you as you come in, and a blessing on you as you go out.
May the Lord deliver up to you the enemies who attack you, and let them be put to rout before you. Though they come out against you by one way, they will flee before you by seven.
May the Lord grant you a blessing in your granaries and on all your labours; may the Lord your God bless you in the land which he is giving you.
The Lord will establish you as his own holy people, as he swore to you, provided you keep the commandments of the Lord your God and conform to his ways.

Deuteronomy 28.1-9

229 Lord our God,
maker of heaven and earth,
your glory is all around us
in all things bright and beautiful to behold.
Your hand is in the wonders of nature,
your purpose in the very matter of creation.

Lord our God,
redeemer of the world,
your love for us is plain to see and know.
Your providence is clear
as nature's bounty supplies our needs.

Lord our God,
giver of life,
your creation teems with life.
Each springtime showers profusion of new life,
and summer yields abundant fruit.

Lord our God,
maker of heaven and earth,
redeemer of the world,
giver of life,
we gather to give you praise.

230 The earth is the Lord's!
We worship our Creator God
with praise and thanks
for the beauty and bounty of creation.
We worship our Saviour God
with praise and thanks
for the love that makes and mends.
We worship our sustaining God
with praise and thanks
for the power that transforms and unites.
The earth is the Lord's
And everything in it!
We worship our Creator God,
Father, Son and Holy Spirit.

231 Spirit of God, at the dawn of creation
you blew over the oceans which covered the earth
and breathed life into humanity.
Blow through our church now,
creating order and beauty
from the confusion of our life.
Breathe new life into us
and make us your new people.

232 God of the sunshine and the darkness,
Of grey clouds and driving autumn rain,
We praise you.
God of the cow in the field,
The cat on the window-ledge,
And the worm on the pavement,
We praise you.
For the breath in our lungs,
The blood in our veins,
And the delicate mechanisms
That keep us alive,
We praise you and we thank you,
O Lord our God.

Enliven our joy.
May we be astounded at all you have done,
And all we know you to be.
May we praise you with all that we are,
And place your name on the front door of our lives.

Above all, we praise you for Jesus Christ,
Who came to us
Like a lover who could not bear to be apart;
Who brought us home
And introduced us to you as you really are;
Who died that we might die with him,
And lives that we might live with you
In awe, wonder,
Love and praise.
The glory is yours, our Lord God,
Now and always.

233 Mother God, you are a God of beauty.
Your creation declares it:
Sunset and rainbow; mountain and sea;
Lake and meadow; blossom and bird;
All declare
Our God is a God of beauty.
Beautiful God, we worship you.

Father God, you are a God of bounty.
Your creation declares it:
Plants and trees; rocks and seas;
Birds and fish; animals and insects;
The harvest of food; the harvest of resources;
All declare
Our God is a God of bounty.
Bountiful God, we worship you.

Father, Mother God, you are a God of love.
Your creation declares it:
Man and woman, made by love, for love;
Free to sin, yet redeemed by love;
Made whole by love;
All this declares
Our God is a God of love.
Loving God, we worship you.

234

The earth is full of your glory, O God.
The skylark sings your praises.
The leaping lamb is your joy.
The dark hills reflect your constancy,
and the changing tides your faithfulness.
But,
beneath the feather, the claw;
beside the pool, pollution.
The delicate snowflake
pierces the new-born lamb like a knife.

We need to acknowledge, O Lord,
that all is not perfect in this garden of your creating.

235 Loving God,
We are sorry that we have marred the beauty of your world
 with the sores of pollution, the scars of greedy abuse.
We are sorry that we have been poor stewards of its bounty,
 heedlessly plundering its natural resources
 and selfishly hoarding its wealth.
We are sorry that we have not treated your creation with respect,
 that we have taken and taken with no thought for tomorrow.
We are sorry that we do not act as your true children
 towards the world that you have made and towards one another.
Loving God, you have the power and the will
Not only to create, but to re-create.
Re-create your loving image within us,
That we might strive with you
For the healing of all creation.
In the name of your Son, Jesus Christ, our Saviour,
Who died that all might be made new.

236 In creation you have provided a rich feast
for taste and smell,
sight and touch and hearing.
In your generosity you offer enough, and more, for all.

And we have helped ourselves.
We have taken what we needed,
and come back for more.
The more we have taken,
the more we have wanted.
Our greed has spoiled creation:
 disrupted the cycle of the natural world;
 brought others to hunger;
 and robbed the next generation of their inheritance.

We confess that our constant plundering of creation
has not given us the pleasure we expected,
and has undermined our well-being.
Forgive us,
and teach us how to live in harmony
with each other
and with creation
so that all may find fulfilment.

237 Creator God,
Out of nothing you created everything.
You called into being our living planet:
Our home and place of journeying,
Awesome in its beauty and grandeur,
Generous in providing for your creatures.
We thank you, Creator God, for the world.

You called into being humankind, in your image,
Man and woman, to be loved and to show love.
You breathed into us the breath of life,
And you gave us a reason for living.
We thank you, Creator God, for humankind.

You called into being prophets of your word,
To call us back to your loving way of living;
For although we reject and betray you,
You remain faithful.
We thank you, Creator God, for your steadfast love.

You came as the eternal Word, in Christ.
When we remained sinfully deaf to your call,
He died and rose again to make us see
The triumphant and transforming power of love.
We thank you, Creator God, for making us a new creation.

238 Let us pray for God's creation – the world in which we live.
Think of:
areas spoiled and laid waste by human greed;
the over-turning of nature's delicate balance;
the poisoning of land and air and sea;
the extinction of many unique species.
Creator God, teach us truly to care for your creation.

Let us pray for God's creation – humankind of which we are a part.
Think of:
those made needy by the greed of others;
the hungry, the homeless and the destitute;
human relationships poisoned by war and hatred;
those who are sick in body, mind or soul.
Creator God, teach us truly to care for your creation.

Let us pray for God's creation – the Church of which we are members.
Think of:
its people, treading the path of self-giving love,
often doubtful and discouraged and confused.
Cleansed, united and encouraged by your Spirit,
may we spread the word of new life for all.
Creator God, teach us truly to care for your creation.
In Christ's name

239 Eternal God, Originator of all that we see and know.
You set the universe in its course and sustain it in its life.
We bring to you our worries, hopes and fears for your creation, our home.

We are worried because the natural order is threatened by the way we live.
We pray for protest groups – Greenpeace, Friends of the Earth, *and others ...*
We pray for government departments charged with the care of the environment.
We pray for international organizations with responsibility for conservation.
Strengthen our determination to change ways of life which threaten your creation.

We are worried because we misuse the creative powers you have given us.
Rather than create beauty, we improve our ability to spoil and destroy.
We pray for artists, musicians, poets and dramatists,
for architects and planners, for researchers and innovators
and for that creative spirit which is in all of us.
Help us to shape ways of living together which enrich everyone
and everything.

We are glad because in Jesus we see you creating the Kingdom among us.
Help us to work with you, that *'the universe, everything in heaven and on earth, might be brought into a unity in Christ.'*

Ephesians 1.10

240 You give us a world to enjoy;
we want to live responsibly in it.
You give us the raw materials of life;
we want to create a life which is good.
You give us skills, talents and abilities;
we want to use them for the good of all.
Lord, turn our wanting into longing, and our longing into action.

241 Lord, you have given us a special responsibility
To be good stewards of the world you have made;
To protect and nurture, to use but not abuse.
And you have given us a special responsibility
To be good servants to the whole of humankind;
To love and to care for and to share with all.

Lord, these are very big responsibilities,
But with the help of your Holy Spirit,
We will shoulder them.
We will be co-creators with you
Of your ever-living Kingdom
Of love and peace and joy.

242 Not ours, O Lord, but yours;
The earth belongs to you.

We mine the copper, gold and iron,
We take the minerals from the earth,
Coal, wood and water; soil and clay.
We use these gifts from day to day
But
Not ours, O Lord, they're yours;
The earth belongs to you.

From orchard tree and soft brown earth,
From bush and cane, from branch and stalk,
From rivers, seas and grinding mill,
We take all good things as we will
But
Not ours, O Lord, they're yours;
The earth belongs to you.

We marvel at the swelling seas,
We gaze into the night-time sky,
By painter's brush or poet's tongue
We think they all to us belong
But
Not ours, O Lord, they're yours;
The earth belongs to you.

243 We listen
for your word speaking,
gracious God.
We listen for it
falling on us like rain or snow,
watering the soil of our souls.
And, when we hear it,
we pray that we may respond.
In Christ's name.

244 The sun rises and sets,
  but your love, O God, ever rises, never sets.
The tides ebb and flow,
  but your compassion, O God, never drains away.
The seasons turn in procession,
  but your faithfulness, O God, never grows cold.

We bring to you all we are,
and all we yet might be,
and offer ourselves
as living sacrifices of praise.
In the name of Jesus Christ, our Lord.

245 Ours is the sunlight,
ours is the morning,
ours is the rain to give the sweet life.
  Ours is all this to see and know, Lord God,
  but it is you who make it so.
  You are the Creator – Maker and Minder –
  for you we would live.

Ours is the new dawn,
ours is the fresh start,
ours is the new song.
  Ours is all this to have and hold, Lord God,
  but it is you who make it so.
  You are the Redeemer – Forgiver and Fulfiller –
  for you we would live.

Ours is the elation,
ours is the fruitful seasons' turning,
ours is the sense of completeness.
    Ours is all this to feel and show, Lord God,
    but it is you who make it so.
    You are the Inspirer – Guide and Companion –
    for you we would live.

246 Gracious God,
in the bright, multi-coloured glory of creation,
and the heartbeat rhythm of the seasons,
we live in the light of Christ,
our days and ways illuminated by your Spirit.
We bring our darkness and our brightness;
all the shades and colours of our lives;
our winter, spring, summer, autumn
before you now in worship.
We pray that, as we seek to draw near to you,
we will know you near us now
and with us as we go.

247 Creator God, with the brightness of daylight
we sing your praise, and creation sings of your love.
Creator God, with the stillness of darkness
we are quiet in your presence, and creation whispers your peace.
Day and night, cycles and seasons
speak of your rhythms, and give reasons to praise you.
    The pleasure of a garden,
    the rustling of a wood,
    the vastness of the sky;
    all point to your creative power.
The resolution of a long-term problem,
the innocence of children,
the composure of the elderly;
all point us to your redeeming grace.
    The love of family,
    the support of friends,
    the depth of faith;
    all point us to your sustaining strength.

Lord our God; Creator, Redeemer, Sustainer of all,
we praise you for every way in which you reveal yourself.
Forgive us when, bound up in ourselves,
 we miss the pointers you show,
 ignore the glimpses of revelation
 and the reflections of glory,
 and so fail to let your glory shine in our lives.
This day, Lord,
fill us with your love and light,
and refresh us by your creative power.

248 Gracious God,
we are sorry that we have not always lived
the way you call us to be.
We have squandered time and chances
to serve you and others.
We have said, thought and done
that which hurt others and harmed their lives.
Forgive us for our hardness of heart,
like the cold earth of winter.
Renew within us, we pray,
a spring growth of compassion.
Bathe us, we pray,
with your warming sun of forgiveness,
that we might grow and flourish
and bear summer fruits of love in action.

249 Origin of the universe, who created order out of chaos,
forgive us for the mess and muddle we leave behind
when we tamper with your handiwork.

Designer God, who patterned beauty and garlanded the earth,
forgive us our clumsiness and confusion
when we try to improve on your skilful craft.

Creator God, whose love called all life into being,
forgive our arrogance and conceit
when we lightly treat the life that you have given.

250 Creator God,
in your hands is the gift of time.
You give to our lives rhythm and flow:
  a time to be born and a time to die;
  a time to plant and a time to reap;
  a time to break down and a time to build;
  a time to weep and a time to laugh;
  a time to mourn and a time to dance;
  a time to seek and a time to lose;
  a time to keep and a time to discard;
  a time to tear and a time to sew;
  a time to speak and a time to be silent;
  a time to love and a time to hate.

For everything you provide a season.
And here we are
all living through differing experiences,
some of us sad, some of us celebrating,
some of us wounded, some of us active,
some of us failing, some of us succeeding,
yet all of us dependent
on your gifts of life and love,
and all of us dependent
on each other's compassion and energy.

In every season, make us grateful;
in every season, make us humble;
in every season, make us aware of one another;
in every season, keep us in touch with you,
the spring of life,
the goal of our journey,
the provider of Jesus Christ;
man for all seasons,
and Lord of our days.

251 God of change,
You who gave us the seasons,
Ups and downs, days and nights,
Life and death, growth and decay,
We are glad you do not insist that we are static;
Immovable, like concrete.
Instead, you made us for variety, for response,
To act and react to change around us –
Not as unfeeling automatons,
But as real people.

So we thank you for the swing of moods,
And the surge of feelings,
For both the highs and lows,
For rocket flights of joy
And dark basements of despair.
You understand when life gets on top of us,
When we hit rock-bottom.
You understand when tiredness bends us until we snap,
You understand when we are frustrated, hurt,
Or just plain fed up.

And we are relieved that it is then,
When we need you most of all,
That you do not fold your arms, looking down your nose,
And insist that we display the right feelings
Before you accept us,
But you take us, you hold us,
You undo the straps of pain and frustration
And let them fall at your feet.

So we bring all to you, Lord,
Knowing that you care,
And look to you for the strength to continue.
This day, and every day,
Speak words of peace, and give us rest.

252 We greet the dawning of the day with wonder.
The birds sing their chorus,
the sun rises high in the heavens,
the beauty, tenderness and strength of creation are plain to see.
God of Creation, we thank you for the day.

The sun shines its rays; light-giving, life-giving:
showing everything with clarity, and warming the cold earth.
And your Son, Jesus Christ,
is light and life for us
over the darkness of our sin,
warming cold and hardened hearts.
God of Redemption, we thank you for your Son.

253 Gracious God, we pray for your Church and for the world.
We pray for the Church:
may we never neglect our calling to a partnership in creation,
bringing fruit from the earth, and light into lives.

We pray for the world:
for those who, by the sweat of their brows,
produce the food we need to live;
for those who, through the turning cycle of the seasons,
work to yield a harvest.
And wider go our prayers:
for voiceless, disregarded workers who learn misery at the hands of others;
for those who are in power,
that they lead wisely, justly, and with compassion.
So may the harvest of the land, and the harvest of justice
be plentiful and life-giving.

254 Merciful God,
how powerful are the symbols for faith we find in nature.
We rejoice that autumn's decay and winter's death
are warmed by spring's hope into summer's fruit.
So may it be for lives
caught in the cold seasons of spiritual sorrow.

255 As we bathe in the light and warmth of the summer's sun dawning each day on us, so we remember, gracious God, your Son, Jesus Christ, our Lord, the light of the world, risen from the darkness of death.

As springtime heralds a new beginning, so we remember, gracious God, that Jesus' call is to a fresh start, released from the darkness of sin.

As summer's warmth gives way in the end to winter's chill, so we remember, gracious God, that your care for us never cools, your forgiveness never dies and falls away like autumn leaves. In you we trust; faithful through and through.

Lord of all seasons, we commit ourselves, as each day dawns, as followers of our Saviour, Jesus Christ.

256 Springtime God,
coming alive within us, like pale shoots thrusting through frozen earth,
we need your persistent love
to disturb the impacted soil of our hearts' rigidity.

Summer God,
growing luxuriantly, blossoming with heady scents,
holding us in your warm embrace,
we need the times of perceived presence
to draw upon in cooler seasons.

Autumn God,
falling and dying in Christ, and etched with the colours of vulnerability,
we need the fellowship of your wounds
to dignify our brokenness.

Winter God,
dormant and distant, starkly challenging our self-absorption,
we need your austerity
to nudge us into warm compassion for your suffering ones.

257 All-season God,
year-round in love and care;
you are the springtime of our every day,
the summer of life's constant bounty,
the autumn of imagination's fruitfulness,
and the winter of our rest and peace.
We praise you.

Each prayer on the next eight pages has been written specifically for one season of the year: spring, summer, autumn or winter.

Spring

258 God of all creation,
as springtime dawns,
we thank you for shoots and signs of life,
for blue skies and the hope of summer,
for longer daylight and brighter colours.

As we worship, loving God,
give a springtime spirit to our praise.
Let the rising sap enliven our worship.
Give the deadened branches of our faith a new life.
Then we will follow Jesus; ever rising, ever new.

259 Dying, rising God,
in Jesus,
new-born lamb,
you give us a sign of your eternal hope
for the universe.

The darkness of winter nights
does not hold the victory;
the stark branches of the trees
are merely transient signs of death;
the chilled bones and frozen spirits
are beginning to melt.

Your gift of spring
cannot be held back.
Through it you provide for us
a sure and certain promise
that your life is eternal,
for in the winter wilderness
flowers will bloom,
and out of cold sadness
will break forth buds of possibility.

So may our spirits be resurrected
and our confidence be awakened;
may our eyes be raised to see our neighbour's need
and our arms be eager to embrace the fallen.

May the Church of Jesus reflect his risen splendour:
addressing the world's pain with positive action;
walking in step with confused Emmaus travellers;
inviting despondent fishermen to eat breakfast.

Forgive us
for the sleep of apathy,
the hibernation of fearfulness,
the cowardice of pessimism.

Convince us that your new life
is available in abundance,
especially
when we feel trapped in winter's darkness
or weighed down by the fear of endings.
We ask this
through Jesus Christ,
our Risen Friend.

Summer

260 Gracious God,
from the rising of the sun to its setting,
you are God.
Your mercy streams over all the earth.
Like the summer sun
you pour your forgiveness upon us
without reserve.

All nations bask in your rays;
all peoples share your blessings;
all the world's children
are equally loved and valued by you.

Forgive us for imagining that we are your favourites;
for expecting special treatment;
for thinking we deserve extra benefits.

Help your Church to be as inclusive as you are,
as all-embracing as your love is.
Give us breadth of compassion,
  openness to change,
  freedom from dogmatism.

Show us how to affirm
those whose lives are clouded and controversial,
and not to shut people out
because their ways are not our ways.

Lead us to rejoice in variety
and to say 'yes' to a multi-coloured world,
encouraging the removal of prejudice and fear.

So may your daily-rising sun shine on us all
and your Son, Jesus, be our shining example
of how to share and how to care;
how to forgive and how to embrace;
how to touch and how to heal;
how to suffer and how to die.
In his name, we ask it.

261 Lord, we come in the freshness of a new morning, discovering that your love is new every day.

Help us to rise on the wings of the morning, taken up by the support of your love. May our spirits soar and swoop like summer swallows, lifting us free from the past, making us eager to worship you.
Your Spirit is like the supporting wind, and you are the Lord of creation.
Our God, we praise you.

Help us to enjoy being with you, and with each other.
May our spirits leap and splash like summer swimmers, cleansing us from the grime of life, cleansed to serve you.
Your Spirit is like a stream of living water, and you are the Lord of life.
Our God, we praise you.

Help us to feel your persuasive influence. May our spirits sense your warmth like summer sunshine saving us from cold loneliness, safe in your presence.
Your Spirit is like a gentle, warming ray and you are the Lord of community.
Our God, we praise you.

262 Lord, we give you thanks for the long days of summer:
for bright mornings and walking to school without a coat;
for daisy-chains and rough and tumble, and play-time on the field;
for long evenings playing outside with friends.

Lord, we come to church to praise you,
but we know that you are always with us:
  in the warmth of your love;
  in the light of your life;
  in the length of our days.

Autumn

263 Lord, we give you thanks for the richness of autumn:
for the distinctive smell;
for the brightness of final flowers;
for the extravagance of autumn leaves turning green to red, gold and bronze.

Lord, we thank you for the colour and beauty of life,
in creation, in people, in bright imagination and the Spirit's gifts.
We confess that so often we take your colour
and turn it into grainy black and white:
  with harsh words, bitter thoughts and spoiled relationships;
  with pollution, war and misused opportunity;
  with prejudice and the strong desire that everyone should be like us.
Lord, relying on our own strength we have discovered our weaknesses:
  break through the mist of sin,
  evaporate the cloud of self-interest,
so that we may stand again in the autumn sunshine
and reflect your glory seen in Jesus Christ, our Lord.

264 Lord, as autumn leaves fall to the earth to feed the coming spring, so may the times of loss and seeming death in us become resources for new life and growth. And if the season seems too long, and winter grips our spirit in its vice, give us the patience to know that lengthening days will lead to brightness and to joy, as year leads on to year, and time to time.

265 Wise and patient God,
we turn to you because you are always with us.
You have carried us from our birth
and have promised to sustain us
even when our hair is grey and our lives tired.

Our world is old but not wise
and we plead to you
in the autumn of our days,
asking that you will help us to be people
who remember the past creatively;
the way you have led us,
the consistent way you have loved us,
and the patient way you have dealt with our failings.

When we tire of the journey
and wonder if peace will ever come;
when our energy is spent
and we long for days of restoration;
come to us with hope and encouragement.

Fill our lives with praise
for all that has been accomplished.
Lead us to refreshment
through the delight of worship
and the supportive care of Christian friends.

As autumn leaves fall
and feed the earth,
so let us pass on wisdom and fruitfulness
to the coming generation,
reminding them of our dependence on you,
showing them how to care for the earth,
leading them into paths which are just and good.

May your Church bear rich fruit
through sacrificial service,
so that people may see and taste
a deeper experience of life
as individuals and in community,
a vision of your Kingdom
of justice, peace and joy.

Winter

266 Lord God, holy and mighty,
we come battered by life,
like crocuses in the snow.
Yet we come,
raising our heads in the joy of creation,
offering our hope and concern,
our fear and enthusiasm,
to create a hymn of life to offer you.

We give you thanks for all your gifts:
for the world and its resources
even when we squander them;
for our families and loved ones
even when we take them for granted;
for our skills and talents
even when we underrate them.
Renew us through this worship,
so that the praise of our daily living
may find new richness and harmony
to thaw the coldness around us.
In the name of Jesus Christ.

267 Lord, often we thank you for springtime's surge of life,
for summer's riot of beauty,
and autumn's mellow fruitfulness,
but then our senses dimmed by cold and dark,
forget the marvel of the winter days.
But caught within this season's time, we now remember well
creation's solemn, quiet suspense throughout the winter months;
the careful harvesting of strength and hope, preparing for another year;
the broken stem and flower that feed the hungry earth;
the fallen leaves that shelter early growth;
the cleansing frost that bites disease and blight;
the patient waiting for another year to dawn.
And then we give you thanks that, in the mystery of your larger scheme,
there is a timely season for our rest,
a waiting which is work, a pause that holds an enterprise,
a rhythm to your Kingdom plan.

268 Hidden God,
cocooned in mystery
like an animal hibernating in the earth,
you are not always parading your presence,
shouting to your world:
'Here I am. Here I am.'
Rather you often seem remote and distant,
and sometimes you seem to be absent altogether.

When winter comes
and our lives are clouded by grief,
whisper a gentle word to our solemn souls.
Send it like a silent snowflake in the night
filling us with wonder when we awake,
reminding us that you are amazingly active even in the dark.

When we have to face life's endings
and our hearts ache with loneliness,
gently enter our night
and show us how beauty is not absent
even when doors close
and lives reach their completion.

Let our faith in you
be a warm blanket to protect and comfort.
Let our hope in you
be a clear, shining star on a winter night.
Let our love for you
be a welcoming haven when storms batter our world.

Let Jesus,
whose birth we celebrate in December darkness,
give courage to fragile bodies and spirits
until the light returns.

269 Small birds,
blowing like ash on the wind,
prepare to leave,
as nights draw in
and days are short.

Small children,
bouncing like corks on water,
prepare for parties,
as tempers fray
and tasks mount up.

But the darkest and the coldest time
is also the brightest time:
    O Christmas Christ,
    the radiance around the moon
    is not as fair
    as the radiance
    around your head.
O holy one,
the majesty of the winter sea
is not as glorious
as your majesty.

At the departing times,
the coldest times
of our lives;
at the times of excitement
and the times of expectancy,
at the times of intersection,
when hard choices
have to be made;
be with us,
Prince of Peace.
    Grant us warmth,
    grant us calm,
    grant us hope
    in our journey
    into a New Year.

270 God of the cosmos,
attune our ears to hear you today
in the great symphony of creation.

God of community,
open our eyes to see you today
in the drama of nature's interconnectedness.

God of our hearts,
touch our lives so that we sense you today
in both the beauty and the agony of the world.

271 Lord our God,
forgive us when we fail you.
Forgive us when we forget what we owe you – our very lives.
Forgive us when we neglect the duty we owe others – our every love.
Forgive us when we reject the responsibility we owe the earth – our total care.
Forgive us when we rest concerned about ourselves,
and ignore the needs around us: in others and in the environment.

Forgive us, we pray, and free us to be
evermore faithful followers of Jesus Christ,
evermore compassionate pastors in his name,
evermore good stewards of the rich bounty of creation.
In Jesus' name.

272 Rainbow God,
as long as earth endures,
seed-time and harvest,
cold and heat,
summer and winter,
day and night
shall not cease,
because
you are a God who keeps your word,
  a God who renews the covenant,
  a God who fulfils your promises.

You give us a beautiful and fragile world
filled with colour and variety,
a world seasoned with your splendour.
Yet you also give us the freedom
to make your world a wilderness,
a place where there is desolation and darkness,
a place of ugliness and fear.
And that's what we've done
again and again.
We have disturbed the balance of nature,
we have polluted the atmosphere,
we have violated our neighbours,
so that at the end of the rainbow
there are blood and tears, a cross and a tomb.
  Dress us in a new robe,
  rainbow God,
  a coat of many colours
  so that Eden may not be past history
  but an urgent goal,
  and life may be rich again
  for all your creatures.

273 O God,
the delicate balance of your creation
is slowly being stripped of its riches:
  your streams of living water
  are choked with chemicals;
  your life-giving trees
  droop and die.

Open our eyes to see, and our ears to hear
the cry of your creation.
Teach us its wonders.
Teach us to cherish and protect your world.
Teach us how to live in partnership
with all things,
that we may learn how to live
as one body in Christ –
  dependent on each other's gifts,
  sharing in each other's hopes.

274 Great Spirit,
still brooding over the world –

We hear the cry of the earth,
we see the sorrow of land
raped and plundered in our greed
for its varied resources.

We hear the cry of the waters,
we see the sorrow of stream and ocean
polluted by the poisons
we release into them.

We hear the cry of the animals,
we see the sorrow of bird, fish and beast
needlessly suffering and dying
to serve our profit or sport or vanity.

We turn from our arrogant ways
to seek you again, Creator of all life.
Redeem us – and redeem your world
and heal its wounds and dry its tears.
May our response to you bear fruit
in a fresh sense of responsibility
towards everything you have created.

275 For the Babel-towers we build,
believing our technology and information can usurp
the wisdom of the Word and rhythms of the Earth,
Creator God, forgive us.

For the hierarchies we construct,
and our assumption that other life-forms
can be defined only in relation to ourselves,
Creator God, forgive us.

For the idols we cherish:
for our conviction that we must honour
profit more than justice, expediency more than sensitivity,
Creator God, forgive us.

For the carelessness we exhibit:
for our brash loudness, our heavy tread,
and our lack of fellow-feeling with land, water and air,
Creator God, forgive us.

God says: Forgiveness is yours
when you go and sin no more.
If you would call me your father, your mother,
then all my creatures are your sisters, your brothers.
Love them as I love you.
Peace be with you.

276 Creator God,
we thank you for the beauty and wonder
and complexity and diversity of creation:
for all it gives and promises.

We thank you for our place in creation.
With shame we recognize the abuse
we have helped to happen;
with shame we recognize our misuse
of power and influence
and disregard for life;
with shame we recognize
that we sometimes think more highly
of ourselves than we ought,
and more lowly of others than is just,
and less caring of your whole creation than is right.

Yet still we hear your voice
calling us to stewardship:
to care for creation –
to play our part in its fruitfulness.
We thank you for your trust
and pray for wisdom to fulfil our calling.
In Jesus' name.

277 All-embracing God,
we thank you that your good news –
that life conquers death
and faith overcomes fear –
is for the whole creation,
and not for humankind alone.

We thank you that the universe itself –
suffering now as if in the pangs of childbirth –
waits with us, in eager expectation of deliverance,
and looks forward to a new freedom
from pain and frustration,
torture and abuse.

We thank you that your promise to reconcile
the whole cosmos to yourself
began to be realized in the self-giving of Christ,
whose cross stretches from earth to heaven,
gathering up the wounds of the universe
and offering them as harbingers of the resurrection.

We thank you for the shining dream
of a new heaven and a new earth,
where you will be seen at last
as undergirding, permeating and transforming all things.
In the light of that vision, may we live together now
with hospitality and gentleness, longing and love.

Based on Mark 16.15; Romans 8.18-23; Colossians 1.15-20; and Revelation 21.1,3-6

278 Please teach us, Lord,
a proper sensitivity
towards your feeling creation;
a proper simplicity
in the way we live in our environment;
a proper appreciation
of the connectedness of all things;
and a proper respect
for the shalom of the universe.

279 God our Creator,
whose hands in playful labour forged the world
and all the suns, moons and stars of space;
you hold everything in being
and continue your work, moment by moment.
And you call us to creativity,
that we might share in making and re-making.
As we place ourselves in your hands,
make us true stewards, care-takers, justice-makers –
so that what we offer might enrich the life of the world
and speak of your glory.

God our Liberator,
who with a strong hand led the people of Israel
out of slavery to freedom;
through the hands of Jesus, your Son,
you healed the sick, releasing them from bondage;
and through the piercing of his hands on the cross,
you brought the world from death to life.
Make us healers too –
healers of one another and healers of the Earth.
Take our hands into yours,
that we may touch all creation with your love.

God our Reconciler,
who, in the person of your Spirit, beckons us into community,
guides us into the paths of peace
and inspires our longing to become more Christ-like;
let your hand nudge us into the adventure
of painting new visions, writing new words,
building new structures, and carving new landmarks
to meet the challenges of our time.
As you embrace us, may our hands embrace the world
to find that all our sisters and brothers – all living things –
share the same pulse of God-given life.

Creator, Liberator, Reconciler,
into your hands
we commit our lives.

280 When we emerge from our thraldom
to greed and the lust for power,
we shall again see the Earth as our temple
and the dust we tread as holy ground.

When we stop plundering our sanctuary
and polluting its water and air,
the seas will not run back,
nor will they rise too high;
the mountains will skip like rams
and the hills like young sheep.
There will be a sense of harmony and interdependence;
the one and the many will not be at war.
For the whole creation is the dance of God
and the Dancer will be seen and heard
and honoured and loved for ever.

O God, we surrender to you our hearts of granite;
turn them, we pray, into fountains of water,
that this promised time of joy may quickly come
and we may learn to dance again.

Based on Psalm 114

281 A Litany of the Four Elements

A prayer for a leader and two others

Leader Earth, air, fire and water are traditionally symbols of life. Our 'slavery to sin' has meant that these elements may equally contain and carry death as well as life.

Life I am life. I offer earth
to share between the daughters and sons of God –
soil for bearing plants to sustain the planet's life
and yield bread for all people.

A bowl of earth may be presented.

Death I am death. I take earth away from the many and give it to the few. I exploit and over-use it. I waste its bread while many starve.

Leader O God, who wore our clay in Christ, we confess that we have not shared the land; we have broken our bond with the earth and one another.

Leader Forgive us: we have chosen death.
All We long for healing: we choose your life.

Pause

Life I offer air to breathe:
for the endless energy of the wind,
for birds to fly and seeds to blow.
Air has no frontiers; we share the breath of life.

Invite the congregation to breathe deeply, or use a fan to create currents of air.

Death I fill the air with poisonous fumes which all must breathe, and which claw away the threads of the universe.

Leader O God, who breathed life into the world, we confess that we have polluted the air; we cannot sense the harmony of your creation.

Leader Forgive us: we have chosen death.
All We long for healing: we choose your life.

Pause

Life I offer fire for light and warmth,
for purification and power.
Fire draws us together in fellowship,
around a meal cooked and shared.

A candle may be lit.

Death I use fire for my own violent ends. I burn the forests and choke the air. I give the rich the earth's energy to waste. I deny the poor their fuel for cooking.

Leader O God, pillar of fire and pentecostal flame, we confess our lack of inner fire for your justice to be done, your peace to be shared on earth.

Leader Forgive us: we have chosen death.
All We long for healing: we choose your life.

Pause

Life I offer water to drink and cleanse;
to be the veins and arteries of the land;
I offer strong waves for energy
and still lakes for calm of spirit.

A bowl of water may be presented.

Death I pollute water with the waste from mines and factories, that it may kill the fish, be bitter to drink, and carry disease. I withdraw water from the land and make a desert; I extend the waters of the sea and drown cities.

Leader O God, fountain of living waters,
we confess that we are cracked cisterns,
lacking stillness to listen to your word,
and energy to act on it.

Leader Forgive us: we have chosen death.
All We long for healing: we choose your life.

Pause

Leader God of earth, air, fire and water,
we surrender to you our old humanity:

**All Christ, we would rise with you:
we would be born anew.**

Leader Christ has died: Christ is risen.
We are forgiven: we too may leave the grave.

Adapted from Therefore, Choose Life *ed. Janet Morley,*
a Service for Christian Aid Week 1991.

282 Come, Holy Spirit,
come, renewer of life,
nourish the potential in us all.
In our work and in our leisure,
waken us to fresh opportunities.
In our families and community life,
nurture and inspire our creativity
in all things.

Drive us out of our pious ghettos
to glimpse new ways to witness;
new ways to use our wealth;
new ways to work for peace;
new ways of being the people
you call us to be.

283 Lord of earth and sky;
as Mary did,
I welcome you into the house of my heart;
as Mary did,
I welcome you into the home of my thoughts;
in service,
in listening,
I welcome you.

Like Martha, I'm distracted;
so many calls on my time,
I run here and there
starting this and that;
never spending long enough;
giving people the impression that I'm too busy
for them.

Like Mary, I choose;
choose to slow down,
choose to sit at your feet,
choose to offer you
my ministry of listening.

Save me from feeling guilty
about the kitchens of the world,
the hot spots, the action areas,
and help me to identify with your compassion
and your presence,
there as everywhere.

Welcomed and welcoming Christ,
may all sisters come together
into your presence,
and together eat at your table
the meal you have prepared for us,
that from the kitchen of your suffering
a banquet may be prepared
for all to eat.

284 We confess, good Lord,
how easily we deceive ourselves:
We turn aside from work we ought to do
  and run to jobs we most enjoy.
We say that we must balance work and leisure
  knowing that our lives are already over-balanced towards idleness.
We announce that we will step back to encourage others
  and then give the others the jobs we never intended to do.
We remind ourselves that 'all work and no play makes Jack a dull boy'
  and forget that all play and no work makes Jack a parasite.
We say that we will do the job better tomorrow,
  knowing that tomorrow will give birth to another tomorrow.
How easily we deceive ourselves.
Lord, teach us
  the true balance between work and rest,
  the real value of delegation,
  the efficient management of our time,
  and how to measure work by its usefulness, not its attractiveness,
and thus serve you and our communities with duty and love combined.

285 God in heaven, ruler of the earth,
we confess the damage we have done by unemployment:
the individuals humiliated, and families broken;
the children deprived of childhood, and communities eroded;
the lives wasted:
the vandals spawned;
the idleness encouraged;
the racism abetted.

We pray for a better use of human resources:
by the honouring of work;
by the valuing of each individual;
by the willingness to set persons above economic ideology;
and by the recognition that work gives human identity.
Into our helplessness, breathe a word of hope:
shame us into protest when lives are wasted;
show us how to share the limited opportunities of work;
guide us into restoring what has decayed, mending what has been broken,
and creating a community that values all its members.
In the name of Jesus Christ.

286 We thank you, Lord, for all that has been done
to ease the burden of unemployed people.
We give thanks:
for government-organized benefit;
for charities providing food and support;
for training schemes and new opportunities for learning;
for subsidies in leisure facilities and transport.
Give us a renewed sense of co-operation
in cities and villages;
in factories and offices;
in churches and homes;
and inspire in us a spirit of holy discontent
until we create communities
which value the work of all,
and ignore the needs of none.

287 Creator God,
you made the universe;
whole and wholesome,
each part interlocking in unity.
And we thank you
that you bless human endeavour,
gift human activity,
and receive as a token of love
the work of human hands.

Worker Christ,
you fashioned wood in carpenter craft,
learned a trade from Joseph,
and engaged in the economics of the village.
And we thank you
that you bless our daily work,
honour honest toil,
and use in love
the work of human hand and heart.

Ever-active Spirit,
you were the action of God in creation;
bringing order out of chaos,
brooding over the face of the universe,
sparking light in darkness.
And we thank you
that you bless the searching of our mind,
lift our imagination,
point us to the higher and the better,
and use the love-offering of our creative gifts
for the good of all.
Father, Son and Spirit,
we give you thanks.

288 For sweat on the brow
 and the sense of a job well done;
For the creative urge
 and a sense of new direction and purpose;
For quiet thoughtfulness
 and the sense of discovery and affirmation;
For conversation, debate and honest disagreement
 and the mutual support of colleagues;
For painting, writing and handicrafts,
reading, gardening, sports, every hobby
 and the sense of fulfilment in leisure,
we give thanks, creating God;
source of human creativity.

289 *On the seventh day, having finished all his work, God blessed the day and made it holy, because it was the day he finished all his work.*

Genesis 2.2b-3a

And then you rested, working God.
Six days' hard labour
and then you rested;
or so the story goes.
And the story rings true to our own experience
 of work and rest;
 activity and leisure;
 obliged labour and chosen hobby.

Jesus defended himself by saying, 'My Father continues to work, and I must work too.'

John 5.17

Resting God,
was the seventh day not true rest?
Is rest another way of working,
and chosen work as close to rest as ease might be?
Working, resting God,
thank you for the rhythm of life,
each part speaking to the wholeness of our being;
rest and work in holy partnership.

290 Weave a web of your presence around me today.
Be with my hands as they work.
Be with my eyes as they see.
Be with my ears as they hear.
Be with my tongue as it speaks.
Be with my feelings and thoughts.
Be with the people I meet.
Be with the things I make.
Be with the decisions I take.
Be in and through,
over and under all,
that doing and hearing and seeing,
speaking and making and being,
I may glimpse your glory,
hear your voice,
and joyfully work with you
to create a new heaven and a new earth.

291 When factories are closed and workers sacked,
and the tragedy ripples through a community:
  Lord, hear the cry of your people's pain.

When people in the prime of life are made redundant,
and families devastated:
  Lord, hear the anguish of your people's helplessness.

When young people leave school without a job,
and see a corridor of unemployment before them:
  Lord, hear the frustration of your people's wasted lives.

When fathers, once called to pass on apprentice skill,
now only teach the workless how to cope:
  Lord, hear the pain of your people's lost opportunity.

Lord, guide and alert
  civil servants in government offices, and interviewers in Job Centres;
  managers making critical decisions, and protest groups agitating for justice;
  investors deciding how to use their money, and charities releasing funds;
  that all may serve the common good.

292 Easter with us, bountiful God,
save your people
from the consequences of their sin.
Where there is division, create unity.
Strike the shackles of oppression
from the empty hands of the poor.
Mend the tapestry of community,
torn by our neglect.

Rise within our concrete jungles
and isolated communities,
that we may blossom into life,
sense hope where full employment
is a long-forgotten dream
and live to proclaim your victory
in the power of the Holy Spirit.

293 Wrapped in the arms of God's love,
as a child wrapped in a shawl;
fed from God's very being,
as a child nourished at the breast;
resting on the knees of God's love,
as a child leans against the teacher;
let us pray
for all communities destroyed by monetary policies
which sacrifice society to individual greed;
for all organizations imprisoned by economic policies
which sacrifice compassion to market forces;
for all countries ruined by their debt to us
which makes nonsense of our aid to them.

Mother of infinite wisdom,
Christ of infinite compassion,
Holy Spirit, guarantee of change,
bring us to our knees in shame,
bring us to our feet in action,
bring us to our senses in prayer,
that with you we may all inherit
a new heaven and a new earth.

294 Reach down, Lord Jesus Christ, to touch and bless
young people who have never worked for pay
and pace the streets to find a job;
women and men too long unemployed
and weary of endless applications;
families with three generations of unemployed
and disillusioned by the society we have created.

Reach down, Lord Jesus Christ, to urge and guide
government ministers involved with employment,
that they may never grow complacent;
grant-agencies, voluntary and statutory, who distribute benefits,
that they may always see the person and never the statistic;
protest groups agitating for full employment,
that they may choose clear argument rather than stridency;
churches, charities and agencies,
that they may discover their most helpful role with unemployed people.

Reach down, Lord Jesus Christ, to shape and challenge
public opinion in its view of unemployed people,
that we may never hide behind prejudice and half-truth;
a society dulled by long patterns of recession,
that we may never accept unemployment as the norm;
newspapers, television and all media reporting,
that editors and journalists may use their influence
to promote realistic attitudes.

295 Lord Jesus, close to the workers of your own time, you spoke:
of the fate of eleventh-hour workers;
the sadness of a woman at home who lost the coin of her livelihood;
the work of the sower in the field, the humiliation of a Jewish pig-minder;
and the efficiency of a farm manager.
Help your Church, in this our own time, to serve:
workers for whom regular daily work is a distant dream;
women, low-paid, working in their own homes;
farm-workers, and others left behind in wage rises;
and people whose work brings little satisfaction.
Teach us afresh, Lord Jesus,
the interdependence of all work, the value of all honest labour,
and the right of all to earn their living with dignity and security.

296 Father, even against the odds,
we commit ourselves
to a vision of a society based on justice for all.

Father, even though the night is long,
we commit ourselves
to the daytime of fair and full employment.

Father, even if the task seems beyond us,
we commit ourselves
to the goal of full co-operation between management and labour,
investor and worker, shareholder and employee.

Father, even if others dismiss it as a dream,
we commit ourselves
to build a land where civilized life is shared by all.

Father, even if history is against us,
we commit ourselves
to create a world where the vulnerable are protected, and none goes hungry.

Father, all this we venture,
and this commitment we dare to make,
because you have taught us
in your Son, Jesus,
that death can become life,
darkness can break into glorious light,
and hope can blossom in the grave.

297 Lord Jesus, when you lived on earth
there was no maternity unit for your birth;
your parents became refugees;
you were rejected in your home town;
you shared the life of the poor;
you were tried and executed out of political expediency;
you learned full well the life of the marginalized,
and knew the depths of human need.

Lord Jesus, present with us now,
meet us in our own physical, mental and spiritual need.
Meet us in a world of desperate need:
where mothers give birth without proper medical care;
refugees are herded from land to land;
politics makes families rootless, denying their nationality;
poverty destroys the lives and hopes of many;
and torture and false imprisonment prevail.

Be with us in our worship
to make us more sensitive to our own true needs
and to the needs of others.

298 Forgive us, Lord, as we live in your world.
The hungry faces stare at us through our television screens,
the squatting figure on the pavement asks for money.
We turn away,
preferring not to see,
preferring not to remember our common humanity,
or the link between our plenty and their poverty.
Forgive us, Lord, that we can live so easily with the needs of others.

Forgive us, Lord, as we live in your Church.
The people sitting near us come with tears in their eyes,
and unhealed wounds in their selves.
We turn away,
preferring not to see,
preferring not to remember our belonging together in Christ,
or the link between our spiritual well-being and theirs.
Forgive us, Lord, that we can live so easily with our friends' needs.

Forgive us, Lord, as we live out our own lives.
We try to give the impression of personal health,
fearing that weakness will be interpreted as failure.
We turn away,
preferring not to see,
preferring not to remember that we too need healing,
and the link between our well-being and your forgiveness.
Forgive us, Lord, that we can live so easily with our own needs.

299 Thank you, God, for simple acts of kindness when human love reaches out towards human need.
With gratitude we remember:
the person who calls next door every day to visit the elderly neighbour, does bits of shopping, calls out the doctor, and sorts out forms and bills;
the nurse who, after the demanding work on the hospital ward, gives up free time to treat the feet of rough sleepers in a drop-in centre;
the accountant who, out of office hours, keeps the books of local charities;
the young person who, after completing a course, gives a year sharing energy, enthusiasm and skills in situations of poverty and deprivation.
We thank you, God, for all the people we never notice but who, with quietness and grace, do the work of Christ.

300 Let us pray to God for all who stand in need
and those who work in the name of Christ alongside them.
For Christian Aid, CAFOD and Tearfund
as they serve alongside the poor of the earth,
meeting disaster and working for long-term development.
For Church Action on Poverty and the Churches' National Housing Coalition
as they raise the awareness of Christians of need in this country
and help them to respond to it.
For mission agencies
as they share the good news of Jesus Christ throughout the world,
and especially for the work of ...
Help us to be partners in all this work,
so that it is done in our name and through our love,
as well as in the name and through the love of Jesus Christ.
Let us pray, too, for our church, that we may be a place where people are given time and attention and space to be themselves, where pain is shared and the love of God discovered.

301 Lord Jesus,
you committed yourself to a world
which needed you,
yet rejected you.

We commit ourselves,
all that we are and all that we have,
to the world that you still love;
believing that in doing so
we are committing ourselves to you.

302 God be with you in your reality.
Christ be with you in your adversity.
Spirit be with you in your perplexity.
And may we all be with each other
In solidarity.

303 May your pain give birth to hope.
May you find that dark clouds
Can bring the rain of life and growth.
May you know yourself loved and cherished
By the glorious God who walks beside you.
And may the blessing of God Almighty,
Father, Son and Holy Spirit,
Be with you always.

Christian Life-style

Put on, then, garments that suit God's chosen and beloved people: compassion, kindness, humility, gentleness, patience. Be tolerant with one another and forgiving, if any of you has cause for complaint: you must forgive as the Lord forgave you. Finally, to bind everything together and complete the whole, there must be love. Let Christ's peace be arbiter in your decisions, the peace to which you were called as members of a single body. Always be thankful. Let the gospel of Christ dwell among you in all its richness; teach and instruct one another with all the wisdom it gives you. With psalms and hymns and spiritual songs, sing from the heart in gratitude to God. Let every word and action, everything you do, be in the name of the Lord Jesus, and give thanks through him to God the Father.

Colossians 3.12-17

304 Lord of heaven and earth,
Lord of land and sea,
Lord of church and home,
we worship you
and seek your inspiration for our lives.

305 Parent God,
you care for us with overflowing love.
Jesus, Son of God,
you guide us with all-encompassing wisdom.
Holy Spirit of God,
you inspire us in our life of faith.
Father, Son and Holy Spirit,
receive our worship for all you have given us.

306 Loving God, we come to worship you.
We bring our gifts and we bring ourselves;
we bring our hopes and we bring our fears;
we bring our experience of this last week,
  its hurt and its delight;
we bring our thoughts of those for whom we want to pray.

We bring our families and friends,
  those close to us and those far away;
we bring the work we have done this week,
  and the work we have failed to do;
we bring our relationships within this church,
  and all our contacts in the wider community of town and nation.
These all, Lord, we lay before you.
If anything we bring is good in your sight – affirm and bless us.
If anything we bring is lacking in purpose and truth – enlighten and guide us.
If anything we bring is fragmented and broken – heal and mend us.
If anything we bring is twisted and tawdry – forgive and renew us.
But, Lord, whatever we bring, do not reject us;
welcome us in your Son's name.

307 Loving God, Lord of the Church,
we are your family because you have fathered us into being,
we belong to you because you have mothered us into life.
Help us to live like brothers and sisters:
speaking and listening to one another;
helping each other to grow up;
forgiving one another after disagreements;
knowing that we are linked not alone by our own choice
but by your deciding,
so that we learn this day to praise your holy name
with one voice and heart.

308 Loving God, your care for us is never-ending, yet we fail you so often with our selfish lives.
We are sorry for the times when we do not love as deeply as we should, when we do not share, when we are angry, when we are greedy, when we are turned in on ourselves.
Our home-life is not the perfect example we should be showing to others.
Forgive us for our poor witness to your all-forgiving love which is shown daily to us.
Remake us in your image, so that our homes and our lives reflect the glory of heaven,
for the sake of your Son, Jesus.

309 Father, forgive us the foolish mistakes we make.
We raise children out of your gift of love
and then turn them into pale reflections of ourselves.
We know the purpose of life is to move to maturity
but take offence when our children grow beyond us.
We long for our children to find the wings of freedom
but hold on to them when we ought to let go.
We want to give our children the values that have served us well
but forget that the world has changed since we accepted them ourselves.
Teach us, Lord, when to speak and when to be silent;
when to move forward and when to stand back;
when to declare our own beliefs and when to leave the moment to your Spirit.
And more, when to influence and when to let our children influence us;
when to teach and when to know that we have become learners again;
and all this for their growth,
and ours.

310 Eternal God,
For the beauty of creation
We praise you.
With the un-named longings of our hearts
We come to you.

Where we have denied or ignored your love,
Forgive us.
Where we have broken faith with you and those we love,
Forgive us.
Where your world is damaged by our neglect,
Forgive us.

Take our neglect, our brokenness, our denial
and weave them into a new pattern.
Set us free from old ways.
Strengthen us to make amends,
and help us to live again as whole people,
through the love of Christ the healer.

311 Spirit hovering over our chaos,
help us to acknowledge our sin;
lead us to deeper repentance in unity with Christ.
Help us to admit our emptiness,
that we may turn to be filled
with the love that rushes to meet us.
May we be more conscious of God's goodness
than of our own guilt.
May we allow ourselves to be embraced and kissed
by the father, who delights in us,
and if we look out of the eyes of the other,
the elder brother, in jealousy and pain,
help us to admit our emptiness,
that we may turn to be filled
with the love that says:
'My son, my daughter,
you are with me always,
and all I have is yours.'

When we see the happiness of a father and children
through the smoke of the cooking fire,
from behind the daily juggling act of unfinished tasks,
may our tears be ones of joy,
as we admit our emptiness,
our longing for fulfilment,
and receive the understanding love
which empowers and enables us
to serve by being ourselves.

Based on the story of the Prodigal Son (Luke 15.11-32).

312

Father God,
we thank you that we are made in your image,
so that we can reveal your goodness and glory in the world.
May our lives in home, school or work,
with family, friends or strangers,
reveal your love in all we say and do.

We thank you that you sent your Son to live as one of us:
to enter our experience and share our feelings;
to live with our hopes and fears, our rejoicing and sorrow;
to know the trials and joys of living in a home;
to accept the tensions and the sharing of family life.
May his example guide us in our relationships
with parents and children, brothers and sisters.

We thank you for the fruits of the Spirit:
love, joy and peace;
patience, kindness and goodness;
faithfulness, humility and self-control;
given to strengthen us in our daily lives.
May they be in us in full abundance and so enrich our home-life.

We thank you for all that makes for a good home-life
and enables us to share in your eternal life.

313

God of every family on earth, it's a fine feeling
when everything goes right in a family:
when a birthday or anniversary gives cause for celebration;
when exam results are encouraging;
when everyone is at the peak of good health;
when spiritual unity is as real as the ties of blood.

God of every family on earth, it's a fine feeling
when family fortunes plummet –
yet each member is held in a network of care;
when the world pronounces 'failure' –
yet the family values the one rejected;
when a parent or child is ill – yet feels the family's healing;
when human values divide a family – yet respect and love remain.
Father of every family on earth,
for all our families have given to us,
for all they have enabled us to contribute,
we give you grateful thanks.

314 Praise and thank God for all who give themselves to others:
for children who have learned the gift of sharing;
for young people who have grown sensitive to the needs of others;
for men and women who give time and money
to make life easier for those in need;
for older people who listen with sympathy,
and pray for others with understanding.
May our families become resource centres of such loving;
privilege and responsibility jointly owned;
younger and older learning from one another,
in the name of Jesus Christ.

315 Bonding, loving God, from the many peoples of the world
you have made your Church a new family in Christ.
It is the friendship of Jesus that binds us together,
his love that gives us unity,
and his care that sends us out to serve the world.
We thank you that when we are strong
we can give ourselves to your Church with active strength;
and that in our times of weakness
we can lean on the strength of others.
Taught by Jesus, we have learned
to rejoice with those who rejoice
and weep with those who weep,
so that, as friends of God, we become friends of one another.

316 Father and Lord,
when people seem to hate each other
give them greater understanding;
when parents and children misunderstand each other
help them to listen to each other;
when friendship is broken
show us how to mend it;
when the Church is fragmented
grant your healing touch;
when nations are suspicious of each other
may they learn a new humanity of care;
and, Lord, since we ask these things for others,
show us how to build bridges of friendship in our own lives.

317 Guiding, supporting God,
we have learned many things since the day we were born:
determination made us get off our knees and walk, instead of crawl;
curiosity encouraged us to learn to read;
the ideas of parents and teachers introduced us to new hobbies;
conversations and arguments with friends helped to sort out our ideas about life,
and the gift of humility encouraged us to admit difficulties and seek advice.
And now we are four or forty, eight or eighty, we pray,
keep us as determined as ever, and as curious as before,
still ready to tackle new ideas,
and humble enough to admit our ignorance.

318 God our Lover,
as husbands and wives,
friends and partners
grow through their love,
learn by their mistakes,
and are united yet separate,
so may we be dependent on you,
and independent of you,
and interdependent with you,
that we may truly be
Mother, Brother, Sister of Christ,
one kindred,
one household of faith.

319 For all who are finding life difficult,
people unemployed, struggling to make ends meet,
seeking new opportunities, weighed down with responsibility,
Loving Lord: **Hear our prayer.**

For all who are sad,
people who are sick, at home or in hospital,
anxious for themselves or someone they love,
worried by bad news, or lost in bereavement,
Loving Lord: **Hear our prayer.**

For all who feel unloved,
lonely people, away from home and friends,
families facing separation or divorce,
children abused or ignored,
Loving Lord: **Hear our prayer.**

For all who want a better life,
people who do not like the way they are,
those afraid to go out, unable to make new relationships,
frightened by life itself,
Loving Lord: **Hear our prayer.**

God, you love each and every person;
help those we have mentioned in our prayers to know your love,
so that their lives are enriched and fulfilled, and they are free to love others.
Lord Jesus, who once took children on your knee,
we pray in loving compassion for the children of our own time.

320 For children in their happiness:
birthday parties, summer picnics, winter treats, playground friendships;
children loved by parents and friends;
children secure in the bonds of family life.
These are your children and we pray for them: **We know you love them.**

For children who are unhappy:
children made insecure because their parents argue;
children who don't like their school and feel left out in a crowd;
children who are bullied, teased, pushed to the edge of their group.
These are your children and we pray for them: **We know you love them.**

For children who live in the world's danger spots:
children who experience warfare and enmity as a daily event;
children who have watched their homes destroyed, their parents hurt or killed;
children who have never known the simple pleasures of play and relaxation.
These are your children and we pray for them: **We know you love them.**

For children who are handicapped or ill:
children imprisoned in ill-formed bodies or unformed minds;
children who cannot live active lives;
children whose spiritual lives are stunted
because no one has told them about God;
children ill at home or in hospital.
These are your children and we pray for them: **We know you love them.**

For children in areas of poverty and deprivation:
children who are hungry, thirsty or without proper homes;
children with parents who love them dearly but cannot provide for them;
children in refugee camps or forced to travel long journeys.
These are your children and we pray for them: **We know you love them.**

For adults committed to the care of children and young people:
those who have taken a stranger's child into their own home;
those who work for organizations committed to the care of children;
those who voluntarily give time, money, love and care.
These adults, Lord, are your children
and we pray for them: **We know you love them**

321

Jesus, we are glad you were born a child of Mary, in Bethlehem,
keep our hearts open like children's.
Jesus, we are glad you lived as a boy in the Nazareth family,
bless our homes and those we love.
Jesus, we are glad you spent your youth as a carpenter,
help us to do our daily work with integrity.
Jesus, we are glad you sought out the company of a group of friends,
may we find life richer by friendship given and received.
Jesus, we are glad that people looked at your life and called it 'good',
each day help us to uphold your name by the quality of our life-style.
Jesus, we are glad, though deeply sad,
that by nails and cross, your death has pointed us to God.

322 Jesus,
child of Mary, son of Joseph,
brother of James, Joseph, Simon and Judas,
you grew up in a family home;
may our home life follow your example
of a life which gives everything
for the sake of those we love.

Jesus,
teacher of the disciples, healer of the sick,
forgiver of sins, friend of Lazarus, Mary and Martha,
you lived a perfect life in the company of others;
may our lives follow your example of overflowing love.

Jesus,
radical prophet, penetrating teacher,
you questioned the Jewish leaders, and defied the Romans,
challenged Zacchaeus, and upset people's complacent lives;
disturb us with the cutting edge of your righteous Word,
then we may live only for you,
and not selfishly for ourselves.

Jesus, our brother, friend and guide,
we dedicate ourselves to you.

323 Father and Lord,
remembering that the hands of Jesus
  blessed little children,
  touched a leper,
  broke bread,
  and bled from piercing nails,
we commit ourselves, hands, heart and love
  to the task of healing,
  to the welcome of strangers,
  to the holding of the distressed,
  to the sharing of bread and warmth,
  and to generosity in giving,
so that hands, heart and love
may be instruments for your purpose.

324 Creator God,
you are life;
fruitfulness,
bursting,
bubbling,
gushing,
spilling into the universe
like a river rushing to the ocean;
chattering,
splashing,
eager,
excited.

What name can we give you?
Spirit of possibility?
Source of generosity?
Giver of life?
Provider of each new day?

No name embraces you adequately.
You are beyond our powers to describe.
Accept instead
our silent affirmation of your presence,
and allow our bodies, minds and spirits
to be filled with your gifts of grace,
as you showed us
in Jesus Christ, our Lord.

325 God of north, south, east and west,
God of black and white, yellow and brown,
God of large and small, young and old,
God of Jesus and Paul, Peter and Mary.
God of every place and every person,
  we worship and praise you.
Let the Spirit fill us today:
opening our eyes to see human need;
stretching out our arms to welcome;
sending us on our way to sing and serve;
through Jesus Christ.

326 Generous God,
you are perfect in goodness;
a goodness you make into a gift,
spilling over into creation,
transforming human life;
a goodness and beauty
seen both in life and in death,
  in prosperity and in suffering,
  in joy and in tragedy.
We are filled with astonishment
at the way your Spirit moves in our lives,
bringing hope,
deepening love,
creating new possibilities,
and all because you are wonderful in all your ways
and consistent in your generosity.

God,
Creator, Son and Spirit,
we adore you for who you are,
and for all you offer your world,
yesterday, today and always.

327 Gracious God,
where love is replaced by domination
or trivialized for commercial gain,
forgive us for neglecting the gifts of your Spirit.

Where joy is snuffed out by pessimism
or stifled by apathy,
forgive us for undermining the gifts of your Spirit.

Where peace is destroyed by violence
and broken by ambitious nationalism,
forgive us for failing to use the gifts of your Spirit.

Where patience is paralysed
by greedy demands for instant success,
forgive us for manipulating the gifts of your Spirit.

Where kindness is treated as weakness
or rejected through lack of grace,
forgive us for underestimating the gifts of your Spirit.

Where goodness is crucified by the power-hungry
and passes unrecognized by a noisy, busy world,
forgive us for losing sight of the gifts of your Spirit.

Where faithfulness is abandoned
and no one trusts another any more,
forgive us for wiping out the gifts of your Spirit.

Where gentleness is ridiculed
and people build their lives round aggression,
forgive us for misrepresenting the gifts of your Spirit.

Where we lose self-control,
giving in to the violence of our emotions,
forgive us for not trusting the gifts of your Spirit.

Holy Spirit,
forgive us our rejection of your riches;
open the hearts of nations and peoples
to receive
love, joy, peace,
patience, kindness, goodness,
faithfulness, gentleness and self-control,

but start with us.

328 Holy Spirit,
you are depth, silence and wholeness.
  Into a noisy, tiresome world
    speak your word of calm.
  Into troubled, fretful hearts
    let your peace descend.
  Into relationships fractured by misunderstanding and hurt
    bring your reconciling love
And thus may our faith find depth, silence and wholeness.

329 Life-giving God,
you have not left us as orphans
starved of love,
deprived of hope,
struggling to survive
in a dangerous and confused world.

You are the great provider.
By your Holy Spirit
you bring to your people
resources rich beyond their deserving.

Our praise is unending
for this reservoir of gifts
always available,
always replenished,
never means-tested,
never diminished by our failure to receive.

Our praise is unending
for the people we have known
who have given us a glimpse
of how worthwhile these qualities are
and how they can transform the world,
making it a place of beauty and hope.

Our praise is unending
for Jesus Christ
in whom we see your gifts in action,
your graces lived out
in a life of
love, joy and peace,
in deeds of
patience, goodness and kindness,
in words of
faithfulness, gentleness and self-control.

330 Holy Spirit,
on our lips
speak a word of love
for those who are starved of affection.

Holy Spirit,
sing a song of joy
in our lives,
especially for those who have forgotten how to smile.

Holy Spirit,
put in our hands
the gift of peace
for those who live in places of violence and fear.

Holy Spirit,
through our thoughtfulness
offer the treasure of patience
to those who endure many trials and difficulties.

Holy Spirit,
in our deeds
show the worth of goodness,
to encourage all who believe evil is in control.

Holy Spirit,
enable our feet
to go the extra mile of kindness,
supporting those who are weighed down by their problems.

Holy Spirit,
in our constancy
display the enduring quality of faithfulness,
so that we may stand by those who have lost their trust.

Holy Spirit,
kindle in our hearts
the candle of gentleness,
lighting the path of those wounded and dismayed.

Holy Spirit,
fill each demanding day
with your gift of self-control,
so that we do not do damage to your name as we respond to human need.
We ask this through Jesus Christ, our Lord.

331

Spirit of the living God,
speak again to us
and all your people,
transforming
confrontation into love;
pessimism into joy;
tension into peace;
impetuosity into patience;
sinfulness into goodness;
apathy into kindness;
fickleness into faithfulness;
anger into gentleness;
and
lack of discipline into self-control.

Then
may we enjoy
to the full
the gifts
you provide
for us
and all your creatures
for the
enrichment
of your world.

332

Holy Spirit, heavenly dove, once brooding over all creation,
bringing order to chaos and harmony to confusion;
pattern my disordered life.
Holy Spirit, heavenly dove, once the messenger of peace,
signalling hope in distress and joy in sadness;
quieten my warring spirit.
Holy Spirit, heavenly dove, once witness to the Saviour's call,
sign of ministry, token of God's love;
confirm my discipleship.
Holy Spirit, heavenly dove, ever the giver of gifts,
causing dead branches to blossom and turning barrenness to fruitfulness;
I commit myself in service to you
and your world.

333 Reconciler God:
We need your forgiveness for our failures in imagination:
we lack the planner's vision to see
where a bridge of peace could be built.

We need your forgiveness for our failures in perception:
we lack the architect's sense of how
a bridge of peace might be proportioned.

We need your forgiveness for our failures in stamina:
we lack the builder's patience for constructing
a bridge of peace stone by stone.

In confessing our failures
we find ourselves released
we find ourselves equipped
we find ourselves ready –
ready to be peace-makers:
planners, architects and builders of bridges.

334 Spirit of integrity and peace,
stir us with your presence today;
strengthen us in our desire to forgive one another;
sharpen us in our understanding of different points of view;
support us in our exploring of fresh approaches;
struggle with us as we labour towards reconciliation;
shine upon us as we bring to birth new visions;
stay with us as we translate hopes into highways.

335 I am sorry, Lord:
sorry to the depths of my life;
sorry to the point where it hurts;
sorry to the meeting-place of life and death;
sorry to the place where renewal is my only hope.
If such sorrow, Lord, is the prompt to forgiveness,
if forgiveness is the beginning of renewal,
then in your mercy, forgive and renew,
and I will rise again.

336 O God, forgive us when – in our personal relationships – we lose sight of the ideals of forgiveness and reconciliation, and take delight in feeling aggrieved, stirring up bad feeling, and planning retaliation for wrongs inflicted on us.

Forgive us when – in community and national matters – we lose hope of healing between different factions, and feel that we are powerless, can take no responsibility, can play no part.

Forgive us our apathy, our lack of passion.

Forgive us when – in international relationships – we lose a sense of perspective and project our own darkness on to other peoples. Forgive our feeling that violent disputes and wars are inevitable, and that the amassing of weapons is necessary.

Forgive us, and grant us clearer vision, hope in the power of love and a perspective rooted in your gift of reconciliation. May we know that you call us to be peace-makers: in our thinking and use of language; in our actions; and in our receiving and reflecting of your grace.

337 Out of my pain
I confess my hate-filled days.
Out of my anger
I confess my wish for revenge and destruction.
Out of my fear
I confess my distortion of truth.

O God, who knows us in our weakness
and befriends us in our chaos,
free me from hate and fear;
turn pain and anger
into tools for healing;
open the door to reconciliation
and restitution of right relationships
between friends and neighbours,
nations and peoples,
that your truth may reign
in our hearts,
and your peace
welcome us home.

338

God of our relating,

thank you

for hands across the table,
for hands across the sea,
for hands around the world;

thank you

for eyes meeting across a room,
for eyes opened to different life-styles,
for eyes shining in new friendships;

thank you

for ears that can hear the beating of a heart,
for ears that pick up the cries of the voiceless,
for ears that respond to the pulses of the world.

thank you.

339

The sufferings of the world are yours, cross-carrying Christ;
you bear the sins and shame as though they were your own.

The agony of a broken world is yours, crucified Christ;
you bear its crushing damage as if you had inflicted it yourself.

The anguish of a divided, hateful world is yours, rejected Christ;
you carry the hurt as though you had inflicted it alone.

The healing of the suffering world, tomb-breaking Christ,
the mending of the broken world, arising Christ,
the uniting of the world, ascending Christ,
these, too, are yours in power and love, in strength and peace,
for out of your broken suffering comes the hope of the world.

The glory is yours, and the victory,
and you offer both to us
as if they were our own.

340 Go-between Spirit of God,
we lay before you the scattered fragments
of our individual lives:
both those parts of ourselves that we recognize and acknowledge,
and those parts we disown, and so project onto others.
Knit us together:
enlarge our potential for creative goodness;
transform our potential for deceit and hurtfulness.

Let us gather the fragments: **Though we are many, may we also be one.**

We lay before you the scattered fragments
of our family and community lives:
both those relationships that are strong and enriching,
and those that test us continually, and need effort.
Bind us together:
imbue us with gratitude for the people who sustain us;
and give us a lightness of touch with those we dislike.

Let us gather the fragments: **Though we are many, may we also be one.**

We lay before you the scattered fragments
of our institutional and national life:
both those laws and values which are just and cohesive,
and those policies or practices which create division and pain.
Bring your people together:
give us the desire and fervour to work for the good of all;
and the courage to name and change self-seeking attitudes.

Let us gather the fragments: **Though we are many, may we also be one.**

We lay before you the scattered fragments
of our world, our beleaguered planet:
both those people and organizations that promote 'shalom',
and those which exploit and reap where they have not sown.
Beckon all into right relations:
inspire us to be respectful of everything you have created;
may we oppose all forces of destruction, without an answering violence.

Let us gather the fragments: **Though we are many, may we also be one.**

341 We believe in God: creator and farmer, lover and friend,
challenger and enabler; wellspring and womb of purposeful living.

We believe in Jesus Christ: compassionate and wounded healer,
wise one and fool; liberator from oppression.

We believe in the Spirit: go-between and negotiator,
inspirer and encourager; barrier-breaker, community-maker.

We believe in the community of faith: alive in the aliveness of Christ,
prophetic in solidarity with all who suffer,
celebratory in its hope, work and witness.

We believe in God's Kingdom: beckoning and burgeoning,
dynamic and harmonious, present and future;
in which we glimpse the satisfaction of our deepest longings,
the healing of our most painful rifts,
and the forging of justice, peace and integrity.

342 Take our hatreds: make them into handshakes
Take our prejudices: make them into peace-offerings
Take our arguments: make them into alliances
Take our battles: make them into bonds
Take our misunderstandings: make them into music
Take our divisions: make them into dances
Take our schisms: make them into songs

343 In the struggle against destructive forces,
we will name and admit our own prejudice, hatred and fear,
and focus on the still centre of our love.

In the struggle for right relations,
we will challenge language, attitudes and actions that divide,
and focus on God's Spirit of reconciliation.

344 Holy Spirit of God, guide us, for we would follow Jesus.
Open our mind and heart to his truth;
enliven our imagination to his presence;
excite our emotion to his offered love;
increase our gratitude for his living, dying and rising;
and strengthen us in our commitment,
that we may walk in step with him, our Lord and Saviour.

345 Lord Jesus,
we follow you because we trust you;
  you are the Way.
We follow you because we believe you;
  you are the Truth.
We follow you because we cannot live without you;
  you are the Life.
We worship you because trust, belief, and the desire to live your life
bring us to your feet in adoration and praise.

346 Lord Jesus, your 'Follow me' still echoes down the ages,
so we are not alone this day.
  We come with Peter, James and John who heard the beach-side call;
  with Paul who followed you along the Damascus road;
  with Mary, Martha and Lazarus who began the journey from Bethany;
  with John who followed you into exile;
    and Stephen who dared even death.
And more,
  with Augustine who travelled to England to revive the church;
  with Hildegard who lightened the journey with music;
  with Julian who explored the inner depths of faith;
  with Luther who restored the road by the gift of grace;
  with Whitfield and Wesley who proclaimed your name
    with new-found joy.
And yet more,
for we remember our friends in other churches, other towns, other lands
who are pilgrims with us as we travel now.
Lord Jesus, with pride and humility we join with them this day,
    and follow you;
delighting in our companions who came before us,
glad to be with your followers in our own time,
rejoicing in the promise of those yet to come,
and joining in the eternal chorus of praise.

347 Forgive us when our lives are guided by desires
other than to do your will.
Forgive us when we ignore you,
and lift ourselves high in pride of place;
pretentious masters of our own destiny.
Forgive us when we care little for you,
care greatly for ourselves,
and care hardly at all for others.
Forgive us, and help us to know
that if we are truly sorry for sin,
we are freed and forgiven
and given the chance to begin again.

348 Merciful God,
we have promised to be followers of your son, Jesus Christ.
Forgive us, we pray,
for all in our lives that denies our promise:
  for being slow to care and quick to criticize;
  for being slow to love and quick to despise;
  for being slow to give and quick to take;
  for being slow to stand for justice and quick to settle for compromise.

Forgive us for being slow to do your will and quick to follow our own desires;
for being slow to worship you and quick to glorify ourselves.
Forgive us, we pray, and free us from the weight of the sorrow of sin's guilt.

Speak to us again your word of new beginning:
that if we are truly sorry,
you truly forgive, in Jesus' name.

349 Give thanks to God
for those who first introduced you to the way of Jesus
  and encouraged you to follow him, remembering especially ...
for those who shared with you the teaching of Jesus
  and encouraged you to obedience, remembering especially ...
for those who supported you when the going got tough
  and encouraged you to persist, remembering especially ...
Give thanks to God for Jesus, pioneer of the new way.

350 Loving God, we thank you
for all those who have listened to your call,
followed you faithfully,
served you wholeheartedly
and witnessed to your truth, justice and love.

We thank you for the prophets
who bravely declared your word
to hostile and uncaring people.
We thank you for the disciples
who embraced the strange adventure
of following Jesus.
We thank you for the evangelists
who risked their lives to bring the good news
of your saving love to all the world.

We thank you for all your saints:
for Christians of every era and in every place
who have lived out your gospel
as shining lights in a dark world.
We remember those whom we have known
who have shown us the way of love
and given us insights, comfort or challenge.
We thank you especially for those who have died,
and rejoice that in you we are all made one
on earth and in heaven.

351 Disturbing stranger,
you call and we follow.
You call, and we leave behind
the nets of our past lives;
the things that bound and held us;
our old selves and our regrets.

For calling and disturbing,
for surprising and making new,
for nurturing us towards wholeness,
we thank you, Lord.

352 God of all life, who wills to us all
the power of choice,
and the self-determination of freedom,
in Jesus you have shown us
the possibility of your Kingdom
and the way of peace.
Today you are calling us to be
friends, followers and seekers;
followers of Jesus,
friends of the poor,
and seekers of justice.
Encircle us with the sweetness and strength
of your mercy, that we may choose
to walk the way of Jesus.
Protect all those who tread the path
of danger in your name;
may courage be their companion,
and wisdom their guide.
Overcome our eager readiness
to choose the path of selfishness and death
so that, choosing service and life,
we may journey with the risen and ever-rising Christ.

353 Our confidence is in you, loving God;
you are the foundation of the universe,
mother-like you brought us to birth,
father-like you watch over us, protecting.
You are the source of life and faith alike.
If you were not, we would cease to be.
We your children have rested our hope on you
and sought to follow Jesus.

Yet, even with such confidence, there are times
when faith bends under pressure,
bends and almost breaks;
times when it seems that the family door has closed on us,
closed, and we are orphaned;
times when our peace is disturbed,
disturbed, and we are tiny craft on a stormy ocean.

For we know pain and sadness, frustration, fear and loss,
even when we have sought to follow Jesus.
Our pain, and the pain we feel for others, is like a heavy burden to us:
cruelty and anger, war and persecution,
bereavement and the loss of a loved one,
can bring us to such moments,
even when we are followers of Jesus.

But then we pause before the sight of a cross,
and stay our eyes on a young man's agony in death;
your own purpose in him seemingly thwarted.
And learn afresh that you are in our sadness as in happiness;
in the dark shadows of life as well as in bright joy,
in our uncertainty as well as in our confidence,
for you are walking with us through our days.

Thus we accept afresh the risk and joy of trusting you,
offering all that we are;
past, present and future,
and with renewed delight
rejoice to follow Jesus.

354

'One more step along the world we go.'
For those whose steps are dogged by fear;
For those whose steps are weak and slow;
We pray: **'Keep them travelling along with you.'**

'One more step along the world we go.'
For those who dare not venture out;
For those who refuse your invitation;
We pray: **'Keep them travelling along with you.'**

'One more step along the world we go.'
For those embittered by life's disappointments;
For those finding solace in forbidden pleasure;
We pray: **'Keep them travelling along with you.'**

'One more step along the world I go.'
For ourselves, fearful, hesitant, tempted, searching;
We pray: **'Keep us travelling along with you.'**

355 Christ our advocate,
we pray for our sisters and brothers throughout the world;
out of our poverty and theirs,
may we not stumble
by judging each other.
The one who follows Christ: **Will do the work he does.**

Christ, brother of the poor,
in the faces of our partners may we see your love.
In our faces may they see your love.
Together may we abide in you,
celebrating the risen life of the Kingdom.
The one who follows Christ: **Will do the work he does.**

Christ, bridge-builder,
help us to work with you and for you.
Through the power of the Spirit
help us to rebuild
God's community of divine purpose
in partnership with all your people.
The one who follows Christ: **Will do the work he does.**

356 Lord,
I may not have
the great oratory of the preacher
or the sensitive touches of a poet;
I may not have
the vision of an artist
or the ear of a great musician,
but I will strive to be
all that I ought to be
in your sight,
and stretch my talents and skills
to the uttermost
so that your world is filled with beauty
and my life becomes an offering of joy.

357 All that I am is yours, Lord, all that I try to be.
All that I ever hope for, all that I long to see.
Because of your love, in joy I give it to you.

All I have been is yours, Lord, all that I did and said.
All that I planned and worked for, all in my heart and head.
Because of your touch, in praise I give it to you.

All I shall be is yours, Lord, all that I will make mine.
All future hurts and failures, all sadness, joy and wine.
Because of your strength, in faith I give it to you.

All that you are you gave us. And through all that is given.
We give you all that we are, we give you our living.
In joy, in praise, in growing hope,
In dumbfounded thanksgiving.

358 Lord Jesus Christ,
you have never spurned or rejected
any gift offered
in love and sincerity.

Whether we have brought you
a simple cry for help
or an elaborate act of praise
you have been equally receptive.

Help us not to be ashamed
of simple gifts.
Help us to be glad
of what skills we have
so they are used to your glory.

So may our worship
raise in praise to you
the routine experience
and the magic moments
of our lives.

359 Lord, we have heard you call us,
Heard you ask to enter our lives.
Lord, you are our God and Saviour:
We come before you in worship and praise.

Lord, we have heard you call us
To be your disciples, learning from you.
Lord, you are our leader and teacher:
We come to listen to your living Word.

Lord, we have heard you call us
To serve you lovingly in the world.
Lord, you are the Spirit of life and love:
We come to open up our lives to you.

360 Generous God,
you love me 'just as I am';
no preconditions,
no ifs and buts,
no 'let's wait and see',
and so I find my life fulfilled,
my spirits lifted, and my hope renewed.

Accepting God,
you take my offered service with a grateful smile
as though my gifts were worthy of your love,
as though I gave you what you could not own yourself,
and so I find new powers within myself
to give, and give, and give again.

Challenging God,
you come to me and share your vision for your world;
you show me people I can help and love,
you tread new paths, and urge me to follow as your pilgrim friend,
you tutor me to be your hands and feet,
to voice your message and your truth,
and so, in losing what I thought I was,
I find myself, and what you call me yet to be.

361 Lord, you have called me to serve you
And I have tried,
But I have become disillusioned
With myself, with others, and with your way of love,
So that now I try to ignore your promptings
To show love, to offer care.

Sometimes I have neglected and angered those who love me
By spending too much time loving others;
Sometimes I have become over-tired and stressed
Attempting to do more than I can.
Things do not always work out as I would wish;
My loving words and actions are misconstrued
Or treated with suspicion.
I lose my patience with those I am trying to help,
Or with whom I work,
And I feel I am letting you down.
I get frustrated with the system
And feel that love has little power
To really put things right.

Lord, you have called me to serve you
And I have tried,
But I have become disillusioned.

Lord, I know that my way of seeing things
Is not yours.
Remind me again that you have not called me
To an easy way of life,
But to tread the path of suffering love,
The path to salvation.
Forgive me, love me,
Fill me with your Spirit of hope and joy and peace,
So that I may do valiantly,
And serve you faithfully to the end.

362 Creator God,
For making the world to be our home;
For making us in your image, to love and serve you;
For calling us to be stewards of your creation:
We praise and thank you.

Saving God,
For coming to live our human life among us;
For coming to break through the barriers of sin;
For calling us to share your forgiving love with all:
We praise and thank you.

Empowering God,
For filling us with love and joy and peace;
For filling us with courage and strength;
For calling us to serve you boldly, the living God:
We praise and thank you.

363 God of justice and compassion,
We pray for the leaders of the nations,
thinking especially of lands where there is
warfare ... hunger ... injustice ...
May those in authority see leadership
not only as the getting and wielding of power,
but as the fulfilment of a calling to serve their country
and better the lives of their people.
Lord, in your mercy: **Hear our prayer.**

God of hope and salvation,
We pray for the Church:
for this congregation;
for the church here in ... and throughout the world.
May we be united in obeying your call
to be servants of the gospel,
proclaiming the good news of your forgiving love
to all the world.
Lord, in your mercy: **Hear our prayer.**

God of power and love,
We pray for ourselves,
remembering those who are sick, sorrowful or anxious.

May your Holy Spirit live in us and strengthen us,
enabling us to follow our calling to love and serve,
and inspiring our actions, words and prayers.
Lord, in your mercy: **Hear our prayer.**
In the name of our Suffering Servant Lord, Jesus Christ.

364

Lord, you have called us
To love and serve you;
And we will.
Give us the wisdom
To know what we should do,
The courage
To keep on loving,
And the faith
That will see us through.
For the sake of your Son,
Jesus Christ, our Lord,
Who died that we might truly live.

365

Lord,
like Moses bearing the agony of the oppressed;
like Samuel in the stillness of the night;
and Amos caught in the rough and tumble of the market-place;
we have heard your challenge to work for you.
Like Isaiah in the beauty of holiness;
like Jeremiah in the swirl of politics;
and Ezekiel in the mystery of symbol and sign;
we have heard your call to service.

Like the disciples at their daily work;
like Paul in the act of turning away from you;
like Nicodemus hardly able to believe what he was hearing;
like Cornelius taken aback by incredible news;
we have been seized by conviction to give our lives to you.

And like them all,
though weaker by far,
and with less to offer,
we respond with love and hope,
and give ourselves to the service of the King of kings.

366 In the clash and clamour of life, loving God,
we come into the peace of your presence.
In the harsh and forbidding pain
so often known in our world,
we draw near to hear
your still, small voice of healing and grace.
Gracious God,
may the peace of your presence
and the voice of your grace
give us power and strength to meet the pain of the world
in Christ's name.

367 We cannot tell
how much the sound of silence,
creation's beauty, gloriously aflame,
moves us to prayer;
we cannot tell
how much the sight of starlit heavens
calls us to praise creation's maker,
and our own.

We cannot tell
how much the son of Mary,
the Son of God upon a tree,
moves us to prayer;
we cannot tell
how much the man of sorrows
calls us to praise the One
who gives our life a meaning and a goal.

We cannot tell
how much the Spirit's comfort,
how much the wind of freedom,
how much the cry of human pain
moves us to prayer.
We cannot tell,
for words cannot contain
the love beyond all loves,
the truth that in the end
there is only
God.

368 *'Father, forgive, they do not know what they are doing.'*

For all the times we have acted without love,
Father, forgive.
For all the times we have reacted without thought,
Father, forgive.
For all the times we have withdrawn support,
Father, forgive.
For all the times we have failed to forgive,
Father, forgive.

For the hurt of the world, of which we are a part,
For the brokenness of society to which we contribute,
For the disunity of the Church, to which we belong,
may God forgive us,
Christ renew us,
and the Spirit enable us
to grow in love.

369 Gracious God, even when the swirl of pain seems set to engulf us,
our thanks can know no end
when we remember Jesus:
entering our world;
facing its contradictions and possibilities;
knowing the turmoil of belief and doubt;
weeping at the tomb of one he loved;
feeling the piercing loneliness of pain;
and then,
paying the price of love upon the Cross.
Gracious God, our thanks can know no end.

370 For the greening of trees
and for the gentling of friends,
we thank you, O God.

For the brightness of field
and the warmth of the sun,
we thank you, O God.

For work to be done
and laughter to share,
we thank you, O God.

Believing
that through struggle and pain
hope will be born
and all shall be well.

371 A Meditation

As winter trees
stretch out bare arms
to a dark sky,
I stretch out
in the darkness
to find the touch of love.

As snowdrops
turn their gentle faces
to the sun,
I long to find
in that warmth
the promise of peace.

As the forest fire
breaks the shell of the seed,
so may my pain
break the shell of isolation
that protects me
from myself.

In the security of darkness,
the warmth of sunshine,
the promise of fire,
may I blossom anew
in the miracle
of your saving love, O God.

372 Living God, you always seem out of reach
but you never let us go;

You allow us deep doubts
but call us to live by faith;

You lead us to great discoveries
but let us be broken and barren;

You offer us abundant life
but tell us it is to be found in places of pain;

You give us an insatiable desire to know you
but only offer a tantalizing back view.

We know it is all for love;
part of the exquisite dynamics of faith,
where doubt becomes the springboard of faith;
pain the fertile ground for growing;
and failure the gateway to new beginnings.

Knit together the fragmented parts of our being
into a tapestry of your making,
that we learn well the ways of your love,
and truly glorify your nature
in Jesus Christ, our Lord.

Based on an original prayer by David Buckley.

373 Loving God,
in Christ you are uncompromising compassion:
  passionately with us;
  passionately for us;
  passionately suffering on our behalf;
lifting us from the pain of our sorrows
and out of the low troughs of despair.

Jesus looked on the crowds
and had compassion on them:
  many hurting from life's ills;
  many devastated by rejection;
  many despairing about their futures.

And we recognize, compassionate God,
that we too are called to partnership:
to be fellow-sufferers with those
for whom life is hard.
Give us broad horizons of love, we pray,
and open hearts of compassion,
to see need and respond.
In Christ's name.

374 God of beauty and power, healing and silence;
haven of stillness in a world of noise,
we rest in your quietness and calm.

Silence

But we cannot stay silent, the calm is broken
  by the gunfire of withering armed conflicts;
  the pain and turmoil of natural tragedies;
  the blare of avarice and careless ambition;
  the tears of hearts fractured by grief;
  the plaintive cry of weak voices begging for justice;
  the whiplash of oppressive authorities;
  the discord of disagreement and dispute.
Teach us how to speak healing peace and quiet confidence;
enable us to share the painful silence of sorrow,
and become channels of your grace, forgiveness and peace.
In the name of Jesus Christ, our Lord.

375 'Lucky to be alive', we tell ourselves,
when disaster strikes
and others fall.
We pray for those
for whom life is a struggle, and never a joy:
those for whom circumstances cut deeply and wound painfully;
the elderly for whom life has lost all its sense of purpose;
and for those facing relentless poverty.
We pray for those badly and painfully injured in accidents;
those marred by natural disasters that seem so un-natural;
those caught up in the crossfire of conflicts;
and those desperately diseased for whom life has become a living death.

Even in the very pit of despair
and the eye of the storm
may your people know themselves to be
alive to you,
embraced by you,
and find the peace that defies circumstances,
and the light of eternity shining in their troubled present.
For the sake of Jesus Christ, who died that we might live.

376 Gracious God,
we pray that we may become the compassion of Christ
to all those who need support;
the tapestries of whose lives
are dominated by dark threads of despair and sadness.
Help us to weave your threads
of consolation, renewal and restoration
into their pictures:
threads of your loving, healing purpose
interlacing their sorrow with strength.
In Jesus' name.

377 Like a thousand springs
bubbling up
in the well of eternal youth,
the nightingale sings her plaintive song:
  peace to the pilgrim;
  courage to the searcher;
  glory to the Lord of the garden.
In the wilderness,
in the common place,
in the heights and depths of our lives,
fill us with hopeful song.
Surround us with signs of peace,
kindle a flame of courage within us,
that we may continue,
with endurance, hope and peace,
the journey that you set before us,
God of all creation.

Written after hearing a nightingale in Surrey.

378 How is it, Lord?
The television screen beams out its light –
  I see the hungry eyes of people far away;
  the swollen bellies, and the fly-infected eyes.
  I do not know them, and I never will,
  and yet I feel their pain as though it were my own.

How is it, Lord?
The newsprint chronicles a further crime –
  a victim's helplessness is there in black and white;
  and pain swirls out in family agony.
  I do not know them, and I never will,
  and yet their pain bites deep as though it were my own.

How is it, Lord?
A casual conversation speaks of family accident and pain:
  a mother bowed in grief, children distressed, a father's anguish.
  The family is not mine, we'll never meet,
  and yet I feel the agony as though it were my own.

How is it, Lord?
Is it that humankind is really one;
life interlocked, emotions joined, our sinewed nerves combined?
And have I touched the secret of the Cross
where pain of all is carried by just one,
who,
rising,
lifts us all?

If so, then let it be,
and I will bear the pain,
and walk the way of Christ.

Offertory Prayers

Instruct those who are rich in this world's goods not to be proud, and to fix their hopes not on so uncertain a thing as money, but on God, who richly provides all things for us to enjoy. They are to do good and to be rich in well-doing, to be ready to give generously and to share with others, and so acquire a treasure which will form a good foundation for the future. Then they will grasp the life that is life indeed.

1 Timothy 6.17-19

379 To the God of us all; the God who gives,
and wills all people freedom;
we pray that our daily giving and receiving,
may be like this offertory,
not tired habit or empty duty alone,
but prompted and steered by celebration
of the love of Christ.

380 Lord, we offer you these gifts of money.
We give out of duty,
and in response to the needs around us.
May our giving also be a sign of our love;
gratitude that you first loved us.
May this money,
and the cash still in our pocket and purse
and lying in our bank accounts,
be used to serve your purposes
by the way we live day by day,
in the name of Jesus Christ.

381 Loving God,
Our Creator, who gives us life and meaning,
Our Saviour, who gives us wholeness and hope,
Our Comforter, who gives us peace and joy,
We make our gifts to you:
The things we have, the time we spend, the people we are.
Use us to show your love to all the world.
In Christ's Name.

382 Loving Father,
All that we have,
All that we do,
All that we are,
We offer to you,
In Jesus' Name.

383 Money, Lord, the love of which
is the root of all evil:
 the desire of the avaricious;
 the motive for the dishonest;
 the cause of cruelty and violence;
 the payment for betrayal.
Money, Lord, the love of which
is the root of all evil,
we offer to you,
for yours is the power of love that transforms.
Take our tainted money and use it,
take our tainted lives and use us
to build your Kingdom
where avarice and dishonesty,
cruelty and violence
are no more.

384 Bless the offering we bring,
Lord God,
and bless us too,
that our money
and our whole lives
might be for you;
that your will be done
and your Kingdom come,
even through us.
In Jesus' name.

385 Take, Lord, bless and use
the offering we bring:
our treasure and time,
our talents and ourselves –
for Christ's sake,
in the Kingdom's cause.

386 What folly, Lord, to think
that we could bring
in offering to you
a single thing
we had not first
received from you,
except perhaps our will to give.

Our lives are the real offering,
freely and sacrificially given.

Bless all we bring
to your use.
In Jesus' name.

387 What evil, Lord, these notes, these coins,
may well have done:
to feed an addict's curse?
to pervert justice with a bribe?
to satisfy a lust?
to engineer a theft?
to buy a gun or knife?

What goodness, Lord, these notes, these coins,
may well have done:
to feed a hungry child?
to dig a desert well?
to celebrate an anniversary?
to buy a needful drug?
to house a homeless family?

Already, Lord, these notes, these coins, have worked against your will,
bred evil and distress;
already worked within your work of love,
caused care and hope to thrive.

And now we offer up to you
these notes, these coins, afresh;
to serve your Kingdom's cause
and glorify your name.

Closing Prayers and Blessings

Peace to the community and love with faith, from God the Father and the Lord Jesus Christ. God's grace be with all who love our Lord Jesus Christ with undying love.

Ephesians 6.23-24

388 Door of the sheepfold, open to your people!
Light of the world, shine before us!
Bread of life, feed us!
True vine, quench our thirst!
Good shepherd, love us with passion!
Way, Truth and Life, give us courage for tomorrow!

389 God our Shelter in the Storm, protect us!
God our Rock, be our strength!
God our Father, nurture us!
God our Mother, discipline us!
God our Life-breath, inspire us!
God our Beginning and our End, hold us for ever in your love!

390 O God:
Be to us the soil in which we grow;
Be to us the air we breathe;
Be to us the water we drink;
Be to us the sun that gives us light and warmth
 and draws us heavenwards;
Be to us our God, without whom we can have no being.

391 You are the Way we shall walk.
You are the Truth we shall take into ourselves.
You are the Life we shall enjoy for ever
 and share with all.

392 As you were in the ebb and flow,
as the beginning becomes the ending,
and the ending a new beginning,
be with us,
ever-present God.

393 Wherever we go,
may the joy of God the Gracious
be with us.
Wherever we go,
may the face of Christ the Kindly
be with us.
Wherever we go,
may the encompassing of the Spirit of Grace
be with us.
Wherever we go,
may the presence of the Trinity surround us
to bless, and to keep us.

394 We have laid our burdens down
in the presence of the living God.
We have been nourished for our journey
in the presence of the living God.
We have taken on the armour of Christ
in the presence of the living God.
Now lead us, guide us, defend us,
as we go into your world
in your name and for your sake,
O loving, living God.

395 You are the Body of Christ.
Go and be hands:
  reaching out to the needy;
  holding the friendless;
and willingly receiving God's love.
Go and be feet:
  walking the extra mile;
  striving for others;
and humbly letting Jesus wash you.
Go and be tongues:
  chatting the good news;
  welcoming all;
and allowing God's Spirit to speak to you.
You are the Body of Christ. Praise God.

396 Go out from here with a pocket full of free gifts
To give to those you meet.
Give freely your love and concern
  as a token of the greater love of God.
Give freely your time and effort
  as a token of the sacrifice of Jesus.
Give freely your help and friendship,
  as a token of the upholding Spirit.
And may all you give and all you do
cause others to seek the true gift
of the God who blesses without end.

397 Go from this place in peace,
and if the walk is long,
praise God – he will walk it with you.
If the wind is cold,
praise God – for the warmth of his touch.
If life is hard,
praise God – for the arms of his love
attached to you forever
by the nails that pierced hands and feet
for your sake.

398 May the mystery of God beckon us;
May the wisdom of God direct us;
May the forgiveness of God heal us;
May the energy of God send us into the world
to exercise justice and love,
and be a blessing to the nations.

399 God of beginnings and endings,
  take the past with its memories,
  take the present with its activities,
  take the future with its uncertainties,
and make of all three one whole;
that our lives may be in harmony
with your Spirit of peace.

400 God, imbue our souls with calm; among us stand.
God, inscribe our names on the palm of your hand.
God, touch us with your balm, give peace in our land.

401 Bless to us, O God,
the doors we open,
the thresholds we cross,
and the roads that lie before us.
Go with us as we go,
and welcome us home.

402 The love of the faithful Creator;
The peace of the wounded Healer;
The joy of the challenging Spirit;
The hope of the Three in One
surround and encourage you
today, tonight and for ever.

403 May the God of all ages, who is the ever-young,
bless, inspire and warm you.
May the risen Christ, a living mystery among us,
burst the tombs which deaden you.
May the Spirit, who is the dance of life,
be your companion and guide,
now and always.

404 As you continue on your way,
May you know that God goes before you.
By the strength of his Spirit,
Share your faith with the uncertain;
Share your love with the unlovely;
Share your presence with the lonely;
And share God with everyone,
Just as God has shared himself with you,
In the unfading blessing of Jesus Christ,
Our Lord and Saviour.

Prayers Before Meetings

Before God, and before Christ Jesus who is to judge the living and the dead, I charge you solemnly by his coming appearance and his reign, proclaim the message, press it home in season and out of season, use argument, reproof, and appeal, with all the patience that teaching requires.

2 Timothy 4.1-2

405 Lord of the Church,
like the disciples before us,
we have been charged with the care of Christ's flock.
May we be so filled with the Holy Spirit
that our words and actions
reflect the glory of God.

406 Father, inspire us,
as we discuss the worship,
witness and service of this church.
May our words be worthy of you,
our witness give testimony to you,
and our serving follow the example of Jesus.
Then our community
and all the world
will know your presence is with us.

407 Lord,
you were the child of a carpenter,
be with us as we think about this church building;
you called a tax-gatherer as a disciple,
be with us as we think about the church finances;
you read the scroll in the synagogue,
be with us as we think about the church's worship;
you healed the sick and comforted the bereaved,
be with us as we think about the church's pastoral care;
you told your disciples to go into all the world,
be with us as we plan the mission of the church;
you spoke of your Father's glory;
be with us in this church,
then we too can show his glory.

408 Holy Spirit, be present with us as we meet together.
We are like any other organization,
with one chairing our meeting and another taking notes,
an agenda to guide us and minutes to keep a record,
discussion and debate to help us to make good decisions.

But help us to remember that we are not here
to decide what is best for us,
nor even what the church might like,
but to discover the mind of Christ
and to seek the Kingdom.

Work through us all
so that what we do here
is not our work
but yours.

409 Lord God,
lead us into your future.
Help us to hear you through each other.
Enliven our imagination to catch your vision for us.
Give us love in our relationships
so that our meeting helps us
to become the people you want us to be.

410 Lord, we are not here
to maintain the status quo,
nor yet to change for the sake of it.
We are here to do your will;
to defend good tradition,
to respond to changing situations,
and discover the difference between the two.
By discussion and debate,
and argument if necessary;
but certainly by love,
help us to do our job well.

411 God, you inspired the writing of Holy Scripture;
inspire us by your Spirit to read carefully,
think deeply and share constructively,
as we look at your Word (tonight).
You have given us wise words
of encouragement and guidance;
encourage us in faith,
guide us in action,
and send us forward
to live by your wisdom for ever.

412 Jesus,
you lived by the Scriptures,
you questioned the teachers in the temple;
you challenged evil in the wilderness;
you spoke with authority in the synagogue;
you pointed out the limitations of human understanding;
you used the Scriptures with sensitivity and wisdom;
you fulfilled them with your every word and deed.
As we read the Bible together today,
open our minds and hearts to hear, to ponder,
to question and so to understand,
and then to live by your holy word.

413 *Your word is a lamp to my feet, a light on my path.*

Psalm 119.105

Lord, as we meet together,
throw light on what we read,
enlighten our understanding,
remove the darkness of despair,
help us to find our way,
and light up our living.
Let your light shine among us and through us.

414 Holy Spirit of truth,
as we meet to read the Bible:

Help us to relate what we read to our daily life
so that our discussion remains rooted in experience.

Help us to encourage one another
and be humble enough to receive what each offers.

Help us to reflect on what we read
so that your Word becomes a part of the way we live.

Help us to be surprised by new insights from familiar verses
and be affirmed in ancient truths.

Help us to find you, Lord God,
in all that we read, say, hear and think.

415 Lord God, make us people of faith!
ready to tackle new ideas with enthusiasm;
ready to wrestle with demanding thoughts;
ready to take other people's ideas seriously;
ready to widen our horizons;
ready to bring imagination to our studies
and thus ready to follow Jesus.

416 Lord, we make no bones about our ignorance;
we've listened to countless sermons
but not taken them in;
we've heard the Bible read, week by week,
but never grasped the broad sweep of it;
the stories of Jesus have been on our lips since childhood,
but their meaning still often evades us;
but we know that there is life, meaning and truth in the Christian faith,
and we've understood enough to want to get the full hang of it.
Please let your Holy Spirit help us now.

417 God; Father, Son and Holy Spirit,
three in one and one in three,
joined together in perfect love,
as we meet together (tonight),
may we know your loving care,
follow your selfless example,
and be encouraged by your divine Spirit:
then we too shall be bound together in your love,
and know you as our eternal God.

418 Jesus, Son of God,
you gathered together the disciples;
an assortment of men, from different backgrounds,
varying in character, in wisdom, and in loyalty,
growing in faith and understanding.
May we, who meet in your name,
learn from each other,
so that we too can live a life of discipleship,
at home and in the church,
alongside the community and for the world.

419 Let us thank God for this home in which we meet
and for the hospitality we are receiving.

Let us thank God for each other
and for all we mean to one another.

Let us thank God for new discoveries in the faith
and for all the resources for study we have been given.

Let us pray that we may use our time together
so that place, people and resources may combine,
enrich and support our discipleship
by the power of the Holy Spirit.

420 Father, help us
to relax and be ourselves, with no pretences;
to relate to one another and to you;
to offer what we have found to be true in our own experience;
and to be open to new insights from the experiences of others;
but more, much more,
to hear what you have to say to us.

And when our meeting ends,
may we know how to put vision and belief
into practice.

421 Lord Jesus,
who visited Peter's home and healed his mother-in-law,
who relaxed with Mary, Martha and Lazarus in Bethany,
who accepted the adoration of a woman in Simon's house,
and who broke bread in Emmaus,
come to this house
and be both host and guest.

422 Lord, hasten the day
when all the earth
shall be as one home,
and all its peoples,
one family.

423 Spirit of God,
we pray that in our meeting
we may learn
so to welcome the stranger,
so to make all who come feel at home,
so to respect difference of opinion,
and so to create community,
that our being together in your name
becomes a sign of the Kingdom.

The following people have contributed to this collection of prayers.

Stephen Brown is a minister in the United Reformed Church and currently serves a local church in Purley, Surrey. Prior to ordination, he worked in the computer industry. He writes, records and performs songs reflecting the Christian faith, in both the folk and rock idioms. He has a developing interest in the writing of both poetry and hymns.
He has written prayers numbered 1, 7-10, 20, 24, 25, 31, 33-35, 39, 43, 50, 51, 53, 59, 60, 69, 93, 95, 112, 113, 118, 121-123, 126, 127, 129, 130, 144-146, 149-151, 153-156, 158-160, 164-168, 199, 229, 243-246, 248, 252-255, 271, 276, 347, 348, 366, 369, 373-376, 384-386.

Kate Compston (U.R.C., with Quaker leanings) enjoys writing, counselling, and leading retreats and workshops. She is committed to 'peace with justice for the whole of creation', likes walking, art, theatre, friends – and good chunks of solitude. Brought up on the Cornish coast, she now lives in Hampshire with her husband, daughter and labrador.
She has written prayers numbered 38, 70, 77, 83, 92, 94, 97, 136, 140, 143, 191, 192, 200-202, 256, 270, 274*, 275, 277, 278*, 279-281, 333, 334, 336, 338, 340-343, 388-391, 398, 400.
The prayers marked * first appeared in one of the annual *Prayer Handbooks* of the United Reformed Church.

Donald Hilton has compiled this collection. He has served as Moderator of the Yorkshire Province and also of the General Assembly of the United Reformed Church. He has been minister in local churches in South Norwood, Gosport, and Norwich, and for six years was Education Secretary of the Congregational Church. He is a regular contributor to the International Bible Reading Association publications and has compiled several anthologies including *Liturgy of Life*, and other resources for Christian education and worship. He was co-editor of *Prayers for the Church Community*, and editor of the *Living Worship* series.
He has written prayers numbered 14, 22, 23, 37, 40, 42, 47, 52, 62, 66, 67, 73-76, 79, 82, 96, 114, 115, 117, 120, 131, 147, 161, 162, 169, 172, 180, 181, 187, 196, 212, 221, 227, 228, 242*, 249, 257, 264, 267, 284-289, 291, 294-296, 306, 307, 309, 313-317, 320, 321, 323, 328, 332, 335, 339, 344-346, 349, 353, 360, 365, 378, 387, 410, 415, 416, 421-423.
The prayer marked * first appeared in *A Word in Season* (N.C.E.C.).

David Jenkins is Moderator of the Northern Province of the United Reformed Church. He has served pastorates in Leeds and Manchester, and held positions in theological training. He has contributed to numerous books of prayers and worship material including *More Everyday Prayers* and the *Living Worship* series (N.C.E.C).
He has written prayers numbered 80, 89-91, 98, 100, 111, 116, 119, 125, 128, 148, 152, 157, 163, 170, 171*, 174*-179*, 184*-186*, 188*-190*, 203, 205, 207, 209, 211, 250, 259, 260, 265, 268, 272, 324, 325#, 326, 327, 329-331, 356*, 358.
The prayers marked * first appeared in one of the annual *Prayer Handbooks* of the United Reformed Church.
The prayer marked # first appeared in *Living Worship* (N.C.E.C.).

Kate McIlhagga, a graduate of St. Andrew's University, is a mother and grandmother, and a United Reformed Church minister in rural Northumberland with care of three churches. She has worked in youth and community development, as chaplain to a hospital and a theological college, and as a Community Minister in a church community centre. As a member of the Iona Community she is involved in issues of spirituality. She contributed to *Human Rites* and regularly writes for *All the Year Round* (C.C.B.I.).
She has written prayers numbered 26, 41, 71, 81, 84* 85-87, 99, 108-110, 124*, 132, 137, 139, 142, 173, 182*, 183*, 193-195, 197, 198, 214, 234, 269, 273, 282*, 283, 290, 292*, 293*, 310, 311, 318, 337, 351, 354, 355*, 367, 368, 370, 371, 377, 392-394, 401, 402.
The prayers marked * first appeared in one of the annual *Prayer Handbooks* of the United Reformed Church.

David Moore has worked as a Methodist Minister in Wales, London, and Bradford. He is at present the City Centre Chaplain in Milton Keynes. Much of his work has been at, or beyond, the edge of the institutional Church. Dominating his interests is sculpture and he longs to carve wood all day!
He has written prayers numbered 6, 21*, 27, 45, 58, 68, 88, 352, 372, 379, 403.
The prayer marked * first appeared in *West Yorkshire Methodist Synod Book* No. 8.

Christine Odell is married to Peter Sheasby, and they live near Ilkley, West Yorkshire with their daughter, Anna. Christine read theology at Lady Margaret Hall, Oxford, and is a Methodist local preacher. She has published a number of prayers and meditations, and a volume of prayers of intercession.
She has written prayers numbered 16, 29, 44, 57, 65, 134, 135, 141, 204, 206, 208, 210, 213, 230, 233, 235, 237, 238, 241, 350, 359, 361-364, 381-383.

Simon Oxley is Executive Secretary for the World Council of Churches. He is a Baptist minister who has served in local churches and ecumenical appointments in the north-west of England, and for eight years was General Secretary of the National Christian Education Council. He has written regularly for the International Bible Reading Association and for *Partners in Learning*.
He has written prayers numbered 5, 17, 61, 103-105, 216, 218, 220, 225, 231, 236, 239, 240, 297-301, 408, 409, 413, 414, 419, 420.

Peter Sheasby is a Methodist Minister, trained at Hartley Victoria College, Manchester, and serving in the Ilkley Circuit. Married to Christine (Odell), his interests are worship and pastoral care. He has written and edited prayers for the Epworth Press and West Yorkshire Methodist District.
He has written prayers numbered 3, 4, 18, 28, 106, 107, 215, 217, 219, 222-224, 226, 304, 305, 308, 312, 319, 322, 405-407, 411, 412, 417, 418.

Simon Walkling is minister of Christ Church United Reformed Church, Rhyl, which is his first pastorate. Before training he was a buyer for Lucas, and was also involved in various aspects of church youth work. He seeks to blend traditional styles of worship with more activity-based and visual forms.
He has written prayers numbered 11-13, 15, 19, 30, 32, 46, 48, 49, 54-56, 63, 64, 72, 78, 101, 102, 133, 138, 247, 258, 261-263, 266, 380.

Prayers numbered 2, 36, 232, 251, 302, 303, 357, 395-397, 404 were written by **Duncan L. Tuck**, a United Reformed Church Minister in Lowestoft.

Prayer number 399 was written by **Ann Buckroyd**, Superintendent Minister of the Huddersfield East Methodist Circuit.

Number	First line	Page
281	A litany of the four elements	172
277	All-embracing God	169
257	All-season God, year-round in love and care	156
204	All-seeing God, We confess to you	124
357	All that I am is yours, Lord	215
9	Almighty and eternal God	6
58	Almighty God, the nations rise and fall	34
165	Almighty God, who called Abraham to leave his land	103
128	Almighty God, you ever call people	79
289	And then you rested, working God	178
182	As a shepherd seeks the lost sheep	113
84	As bread is broken for the world	52
193	As the grey wave creeps on to the shore	119
104	As the people of God gather for worship	62
255	As we bathe in the light and warmth of the summer's sun	156
371	As winter trees stretch out bare arms	222
404	As you continue on your way	238
85	As you have been fed at this table	53
392	As you were in the ebb and flow	235
384	Bless the offering we bring, Lord God	230
401	Bless to us, O God, the doors we open	238
158	Bless your Church – here and around the world	100
126	Bless your Church, loving God!	78
315	Bonding, loving God, from the many peoples of the world	193
196	Breathe in time with the rhythm of the earth	120
75	Broken man; Christ crucified; poured-out life	45
168	Calling God, your voice was known in Creation	104
76	Can we, who every day eat more than meets our need	46
355	Christ our advocate, we pray for our sisters and brothers	214
282	Come, Holy Spirit, come, renewer of life	174
216	Come, Lord, and bathe our feet	133
27	Compassionate God, we know we are sinners	16
362	Creator God, For making the world to be our home	218
250	Creator God, in your hands is the gift of time	153
237	Creator God, Out of nothing you created everything	147
276	Creator God, we thank you for the beauty and wonder	168
16	Creator God, we praise you for the immensity of your love	10
247	Creator God, with the brightness of daylight	151
324	Creator God, you are life	198
287	Creator God, you made the universe	177
351	Disturbing stranger, you call and we follow	211
388	Door of the sheepfold, open to your people	235

Index of First Lines

Number	First line	Page
259	Dying, rising God	157
281	Earth, air, fire and water are traditionally symbols of life	172
292	Easter with us, bountiful God	180
87	Encircle us with your power	53
147	Eternal God, Father and Lord	92
310	Eternal God, For the beauty of creation	191
22	Eternal God of wonder, might and power	13
239	Eternal God, Originator of all that we see and know	148
120	Eternal God, with all who have gone before us	73
148	Eternal God, you are a God of good news	93
66	Eternal God, you hold in love all who know and praise you	39
42	Father and God, who else have we to thank but you	25
323	Father and Lord, remembering that the hands of Jesus	197
316	Father and Lord, when people seem to hate each other	194
296	Father, even against the odds	182
309	Father, forgive us the foolish mistakes we make	190
55	Father God, in the beginning you separated light from dark	32
312	Father God, we thank you that we are made in your image	192
80	Father God, you have never left us orphaned	50
420	Father, help us to relax and be ourselves	250
406	Father, inspire us, as we discuss the worship and witness	241
177	Father, our world is crying out for wise thoughts	109
30	Father, Son and Spirit	18
105	Father, today you have given us a time to meet together	62
176	Father, we do not find it easy to retain our enthusiasm	108
5	Father, you are closer to us than the air we breathe	4
368	For all the times we have acted without love	221
319	For all who are finding life difficult	195
288	For sweat on the brow and the sense of a job well done	178
275	For the Babel-towers we build	167
370	For the greening of trees	221
26	For the joy of a fresh sunrise	16
298	Forgive us, Lord, as we live in your world	183
347	Forgive us when our lives are guided by desires	210
132	From the corners of the world	82
108	Gather us, O God, that we may come expectant to worship	63
326	Generous God, you are perfect in goodness	199
360	Generous God, you love me 'just as I am'	216
47	Give thanks to God, because he is God	27
349	Give thanks to God for those who first introduced you to the way	210
397	Go from this place in peace	237
396	Go out from here with a pocket full of free gifts	237

Number	First line	Page
340	Go-between Spirit of God	207
302	God be with you in your reality	185
110	God, Creator, Enfolder, Sustainer, we come to you	64
61	God eternal, all-knowing, and total love	36
400	God, imbue our souls with calm	238
285	God in heaven, ruler of the earth	176
11	God is love, and where true love is	7
67	God of all circumstances and places	39
258	God of all creation, as springtime dawns	157
21	God of all life, of all ages, of all places	13
352	God of all life, who wills to us all	212
14	God of beauty and power	8
374	God of beauty and power, healing and silence	224
399	God of beginnings and endings	237
251	God of change, You who gave us the seasons	154
36	God of community, As you lead us through the crowded streets	21
313	God of every family on earth	192
34	God of grace, forgive our self-concern	20
72	God of holiness and love	44
363	God of justice and compassion	218
212	God of justice, encircle the earth	131
43	God of love, we thank you	25
209	God of nations new and old	129
325	God of north, south, east and west	198
338	God of our relating, thank you	206
33	God of our whole lives	19
191	God of stillness, hold us in your presence	118
270	God of the cosmos, attune our ears to hear you	165
232	God of the sunshine and the darkness	144
88	God of travail, at one with Mary in pregnancy and birth	54
279	God our Creator, whose hands in playful labour	170
136	God our Healer, in sorrow and shame	83
318	God our Lover, as husbands and wives	194
389	God our Shelter in the Storm, protect us!	235
100	God, present, available, active, welcoming	61
40	God, the world is puffed up with over-weening pride	23
98	God, you have given us this day	60
411	God, you inspired the writing of Holy Scripture	243
417	God: Father, Son and Holy Spirit	245
144	Gracious and eternal God, maker, redeemer and inspirer	91
146	Gracious God, calling people to service	91
369	Gracious God, even when the swirl of pain seems set to engulf us	221

Index of First Lines

Number	First line	Page
20	Gracious God, ever faithful, ever true	12
260	Gracious God, from the rising of the sun to its setting	158
10	Gracious God, give us ears to hear your voice	7
246	Gracious God, in the bright multi-coloured glory of creation	151
199	Gracious God, light of hope in the darkness of confusion	123
248	Gracious God, we are sorry that we have not always lived	152
129	Gracious God, we pray that people will see	80
253	Gracious God, we pray for your Church and for the world	155
376	Gracious God, we pray we may become the compassion of Christ	225
149	Gracious God, we stand amazed that you call us	93
327	Gracious God, where love is replaced by domination	199
31	Gracious God, with sorrow we admit	18
116	Gracious, patient God, you must have wept	70
96	Grant us peace, Lord	59
274	Great Spirit, still brooding over the world	167
317	Guiding, supporting God, we have learned many things	194
169	Hands can fight, and push, and shove	104
114	Heavenly Father, how glad we are to come to church	68
2	Heavenly Father, we willingly draw near to you	3
162	Help us, Father God, to put the gospel into action	101
268	Hidden God, cocooned in mystery like an animal hibernating	163
81	Holy God, for the universe you have made	51
211	Holy God, our ears are ringing with the sounds of voices	130
408	Holy Spirit, be present with us as we meet together	242
332	Holy Spirit, heavenly dove, once brooding	203
344	Holy Spirit of God, guide us	209
414	Holy Spirit of truth, as we meet to read the Bible	244
330	Holy Spirit, on our lips speak a word of love	202
328	Holy Spirit, you are depth, silence and wholeness	200
137	How can we seek the warm safety of worship	84
23	How dare we speak your name, creator God	14
378	How is it, Lord?	226
161	How many people Jesus met!	101
335	I am sorry, Lord	204
224	I am weak – give me strength	138
228	I confess it, Lord God	139
197	I stand. I open myself to God	121
52	If ever, Lord, we meet to praise your name	30
155	If only we could leave it in the past, eternal God	97
236	In creation you have provided a rich feast	146
45	In gladness and thanksgiving we recognize the world as your home	26
90	In the beginning – one God, one world	55

Number	First line	Page
366	In the clash and clamour of life	220
343	In the struggle against destructive forces	208
218	It is so easy, Lord, to pass by on the other side	134
322	Jesus, child of Mary, son of Joseph	197
215	Jesus, full of compassion	133
418	Jesus, Son of God, you gathered together the disciples	245
190	Jesus, teacher, do I hear you clearly?	117
171	Jesus, through your roots in a Jewish home	106
321	Jesus, we are glad you were born a child of Mary	196
412	Jesus, you lived by the Scriptures	243
198	Let silence be placed around us like a mantle	122
77	Let us give thanks for humble and unassuming mediators	47
99	Let us keep silence as we prepare to worship	60
238	Let us pray for God's creation	147
300	Let us pray to God for all who stand in need	184
419	Let us thank God for this home in which we meet	245
51	Life-giving God, we thank you for your Word made flesh	29
329	Life-giving God, you have not left us as orphans	201
377	Like a thousand springs bubbling up	225
86	Like grapes on a sun-drenched hill	53
97	Listening God, may worship happen here today	60
160	Living God, bless your Church in the world	100
70	Living God, host and guest, we await you	43
92	Living God, host and guest, you have been present with us	55
163	Living God, how beautiful are the feet of those	102
164	Living God, seen in the face of Christ	103
101	Living God, through this worship unite our spirits	61
157	Living God, today our thanks are for the transparent saints	99
50	Living God, we are struck by awe	29
60	Living God, we pray for the Church and for the world	36
91	Living God, with all your saints, past, present and future	55
372	Living God, you always seem out of reach	223
111	Living God, you have promised your presence	67
125	Living God, you have set the Church in the world	77
221	Living God, you hold all peoples within your loving care	136
203	Living God, your voice is not silent	124
28	Living Jesus, we praise you because you show us that God is love	17
138	Living, loving Lord of faith	85
175	Lord, a blind and blinkered world cries out for help	108
264	Lord, as autumn leaves fall to the earth to feed the coming spring	160
103	Lord, as we get ready to go into church	62
141	Lord, as we grow older, help us to remember	86

Number	First line	Page
413	Lord, as we meet together, throw light on what we read	243
186	Lord God, give us your strength	115
266	Lord God, holy and mighty, we come battered by life	162
409	Lord God, lead us into your future	242
415	Lord God, make us people of faith!	214
422	Lord, hasten the day	250
188	Lord, I know your commandments off by heart	116
356	Lord, I may not have the great oratory of the preacher	214
109	Lord, in our praise and in our prayer	64
172	Lord Jesus Christ, we pray that we	106
82	Lord Jesus Christ, you are for us our bread of life	51
358	Lord Jesus Christ, you have never spurned or rejected	215
295	Lord Jesus, close to the workers of your own time	181
345	Lord Jesus, we follow you because we trust you	209
297	Lord Jesus, when you lived on earth	183
131	Lord Jesus, where your Church is wealthy	81
320	Lord Jesus, who once took children on your knee	195
421	Lord Jesus, who visited Peter's home and healed his mother-in-law	250
301	Lord Jesus, you committed yourself to a world	185
56	Lord Jesus, you set a child in our midst as a potent symbol	33
187	Lord Jesus, your teaching was given in the language of the people	116
346	Lord Jesus, your 'Follow me' still echoes	209
181	Lord, let silence speak and teach its own truth	112
365	Lord, like Moses bearing the agony of the oppressed	219
107	Lord, now take from our minds all that intrudes	63
62	Lord of all human life	37
283	Lord of earth and sky	174
304	Lord of heaven and earth	189
37	Lord of life, we know you watch over us	21
19	Lord of patterns and rhythms	11
49	Lord of reality, we dare to be honest before you	28
48	Lord of rest and relaxation	28
405	Lord of the Church	241
7	Lord of the morning and of all our days and nights	5
267	Lord, often we thank you for springtime's surge of life	162
271	Lord our God, forgive us when we fail you	165
13	Lord our God, King of the universe	8
229	Lord our God, maker of heaven and earth	143
12	Lord our God, you create and you sustain	7
32	Lord, so often we exploit what you have made	19
410	Lord, we are not here to maintain the status quo	242
261	Lord, we come in the freshness of a new morning	159

Number	First line	Page
15	Lord, we experience you like the sea	9
262	Lord, we give you thanks for the long days of summer	160
263	Lord, we give you thanks for the richness of autumn	160
359	Lord, we have heard you call us	216
64	Lord, we have remembered your redeeming love	38
89	Lord, we have seen your promised victory	54
184	Lord, we keep listening for your voice in the wrong places	114
210	Lord, we know we are infinitely precious to you	129
78	Lord, we lift our hearts to you	48
416	Lord, we make no bones about our ignorance	244
170	Lord, we need a new spirit and a new confidence	105
380	Lord, we offer you these gifts of money	229
53	Lord, we pray 'give us this day our daily bread!'	30
220	Lord, we see you at work in the world	135
206	Lord, we thank you For all those whom your Spirit has inspired	126
46	Lord, we thank you for your love towards us	27
227	Lord, when I see only blindness	139
135	Lord, When we look into the face of someone we know	83
361	Lord, you have called me to serve you	217
364	Lord, you have called us	219
241	Lord, you have given us a special responsibility	149
117	Lord, you made the world and everything in it	71
407	Lord, you were the child of a carpenter	241
17	Lord, your love for us brings a smile to our faces	10
63	Love of the Father, reaching out in creation	38
44	Loving and gracious God	26
382	Loving Father, All that we have	229
134	Loving Father God, we come as one family to worship you	82
373	Loving God, in Christ you are uncompromising compassion	223
166	Loving God, Jesus your Son lived our life	103
307	Loving God, Lord of the Church	190
3	Loving God, open our eyes to the beauty	4
381	Loving God, Our Creator, who gives us life and meaning	229
115	Loving God, present throughout the world	69
235	Loving God, We are sorry that we have marred the beauty	146
213	Loving God, we come to you wearied and appalled	132
306	Loving God, we come to worship you	189
54	Loving God, we come to pray for the world	31
121	Loving God, we give you thanks for our church	74
145	Loving God, we pray we know your Spirit in us	91
350	Loving God, we thank you for all those who have listened	211
159	Loving God, whose living Word is active now	100

Index of First Lines

Number	First line	Page
119	Loving God, you call each of us to ministry	72
65	Loving God, you have chosen us	38
308	Loving God, your care for us is never-ending	190
57	Loving God, your kingdom is a kingdom of justice and mercy	34
208	Loving King, There is so much injustice in your world	128
375	'Lucky to be alive', we tell ourselves	224
194	Make time to sit in comfort	119
225	May our church exist for others	138
403	May the God of all ages, who is the ever-young	238
68	May the God who is perfectly at home	40
398	May the mystery of God beckon us	237
303	May your pain give birth to hope	185
151	Merciful God, accept, we pray, the sorrow we express	95
35	Merciful God, forgive our foolish ways	20
254	Merciful God, how powerful are the symbols for faith	155
29	Merciful God, we confess that we find it difficult	17
39	Merciful God, we confess to you all in our lives that grieves you	23
348	Merciful God, we have promised to be followers	210
118	Merciful God, we rejoice that you entered the world	72
383	Money, Lord, the love of which is the root of all evil	230
6	Most holy, most lovely God, you have called us	5
233	Mother God, you are a God of beauty	145
200	Mysterious God, we seek a safe place	123
242	Not ours, O Lord, but yours	149
124	O Christ, does a mother stop	76
183	O Creator of the earth, save us	113
336	O God, forgive us when ... we lose sight of the ideals	205
94	O God, may this place and this hour	59
139	O God of all youth, we pray to you	85
180	O God, patient and forgiving	112
273	O God, the delicate balance of your creation	166
390	O God: Be to us the soil in which we grow	235
354	'One more step along the world we go'	213
249	Origin of the universe, who created order out of chaos	152
353	Our confidence is in you, loving God	212
140	Our God, you call us to be Church	86
245	Ours is the sunlight	150
337	Out of my pain I confess my hate-filled days	205
226	Parent God, like a mother hen you gather us	139
305	Parent God, you care for us with over-flowing love	189
69	Passionate God, our hearts are stirred to life	40
152	Patient God, we are foolish friends of Jesus	95

Number	First line	Page
277	Please teach us, Lord, a proper sensitivity	169
314	Praise and thank God for all who give themselves to others	193
25	Praise be to you, our God, maker of heaven and earth	15
24	Praise to you, Lord our God – King of creation	15
178	Precious beyond jewels is the treasure of your Word	110
272	Rainbow God, as long as earth endures	165
294	Reach down, Lord Jesus Christ, to touch and bless	181
333	Reconciler God: we need your forgiveness for our failures	204
133	Reconciling God, We come as old and young	82
173	Risen Christ, as ice melts and rivers flow	107
179	Risen Jesus, where else can we go?	111
205	Scarred, battered, bleeding is your world	125
153	Seldom-silent God, we thank you	96
202	Sending God, now that we find the listening-place within ourselves	123
38	Shining, surprising, grace-full God	22
269	Small birds, blowing like ash on the wind	164
195	Sometimes I long to call words of praise to me	120
311	Spirit hovering over our chaos	191
231	Spirit of God, at the dawn of creation you blew	144
207	Spirit of God, like the wind you still move over the waters	126
102	Spirit of God, uplift those who will lead our worship today	61
423	Spirit of God, we pray that in our meeting	250
334	Spirit of integrity and peace	204
331	Spirit of the living God	203
256	Springtime God, coming alive within us	156
201	Strengthening God, thank you for filling our empty hands	123
385	Take, Lord, bless and use the offering we bring	230
342	Take our hatreds: make them into handshakes	208
185	Thank you, Father, for the timeless words	115
156	Thank you, God, for your Word	98
299	Thank you, God, for simple acts of kindness	184
219	Thank you, God, your thoughts are wiser than our thoughts	135
123	Thank you, living God	75
122	Thanks be to you, Loving God	74
234	The earth is full of your glory, O God	145
230	The earth is the Lord's!	143
71	The fire is lit, the table set	43
402	The love of the faithful Creator	238
59	The storms rage, the waves roll high	35
339	The sufferings of the world are yours	206
244	The sun rises and sets, but your love, O God, ever rises	150
1	This day and all days is your day	3
8	This day, as are all days, loving God	5

Number	First line	Page
106	This day, O God, may our lips sing out in praise	63
18	To be surrounded by a world of beauty and wonder	11
379	To the God of us all; the God who gives	229
93	To you, our God, be all the glory	59
4	Today is a day of celebration	4
174	Too many words spoken without thought fill our lives	107
142	We affirm the glory of God's creation	87
113	We are your people, loving God	67
341	We believe in God: creator and farmer	208
367	We cannot tell how much the sound of silence	220
112	We come as a gathered group of your people	67
143	We commit ourselves to the tasks of gardening	88
284	We confess, good Lord, how easily we deceive ourselves	175
150	We confess our sin, gracious God	94
214	We face each other across a raw divide	132
252	We greet the dawning of the day with wonder	155
73	We have heard of one whose life and limbs were broken	44
394	We have laid our burdens down	236
243	We listen for your word speaking	150
217	We look and stare, but what do we see?	133
130	We pray that the Church in every land	81
127	We rejoice that the Church is no mere huddle of the holy	79
167	We remember, calling God	104
154	We thank you for the Bible and its insights	97
79	We thank you, gracious God	49
286	We thank you, Lord, for all that has been done	176
290	Weave a web of your presence around me today	179
387	What evil, Lord, these notes, these coins	231
386	What folly, Lord, to think that we could bring	231
95	What privilege to serve in the sanctuary of praise!	59
83	What we have seen and heard, touched and tasted	52
222	When did we see you in prison, Lord?	137
291	When factories are closed and workers sacked	179
192	When nothing is right, when we are weary and lost	118
189	When the prophets of doom proclaim the end of the world	116
280	When we emerge from our thraldom	171
393	Wherever we go, may the joy of God the Gracious	236
74	Who can sit at this table?	45
265	Wise and patient God, we turn to you	161
41	Word of God flowing free	24
293	Wrapped in the arms of God's love	180
395	You are the Body of Christ	236
391	You are the Way we shall walk	235
240	You give us a world to enjoy	148
223	You have loved us, help us to love others	138

Index of Sections

The Church at Worship

Invocation

Number	First line	Page
9	Almighty and eternal God	6
5	Father, you are closer to us than the air we breathe	4
11	God is love, and where true love is	7
10	Gracious God, give us ears to hear your voice	7
2	Heavenly Father, we willingly draw near to you	3
7	Lord of the morning and of all our days and nights	5
12	Lord our God, you create and you sustain	7
3	Loving God, open our eyes to the beauty	4
6	Most holy, most lovely God, you have called us	5
8	This day, as are all days, loving God	5
1	This day and all days is your day	3
4	Today is a day of celebration	4

Adoration

Number	First line	Page
16	Creator God, we praise you for the immensity of your love	10
22	Eternal God of wonder, might and power	13
14	God of beauty and power	8
21	God of all life, of all ages, of all places	13
20	Gracious God, ever faithful, ever true	12
23	How dare we speak your name, creator God	14
19	Lord of patterns and rhythms	11
15	Lord, we experience you like the sea	9
13	Lord our God, King of the universe	8
17	Lord, your love for us brings a smile to our faces	10
25	Praise be to you, our God, maker of heaven and earth	15
24	Praise to you, Lord our God – King of creation	15
18	To be surrounded by a world of beauty and wonder	11

Confession

Number	First line	Page
27	Compassionate God, we know we are sinners	16
30	Father, Son and Spirit	18
26	For the joy of a fresh sunrise	16
34	God of grace, forgive our self-concern	20
33	God of our whole lives	19
40	God, the world is puffed up with over-weening pride	23
36	God of community, As you lead us through the crowded streets	21
31	Gracious God, with sorrow we admit	18
28	Living Jesus, we praise you because you show us that God is love	17
32	Lord, so often we exploit what you have made	19

Number	First line	Page
37	Lord of life, we know you watch over us	21
29	Merciful God, we confess that we find it difficult	17
39	Merciful God, we confess to you all in our lives that grieves you	23
35	Merciful God, forgive our foolish ways	20
38	Shining, surprising, grace-full God	22
41	Word of God flowing free	24

Thanksgiving

42	Father and God, who else have we to thank but you	25
47	Give thanks to God, because he is God	27
43	God of love, we thank you	25
45	In gladness and thanksgiving we recognize the world as your home	26
51	Life-giving God, we thank you for your Word made flesh	29
50	Living God, we are struck by awe	29
46	Lord, we thank you for your love towards us	27
49	Lord of reality, we dare to be honest before you	28
48	Lord of rest and relaxation	28
44	Loving and gracious God	26

Supplication and Intercession

58	Almighty God, the nations rise and fall	34
55	Father God, in the beginning you separated light from dark	32
61	God eternal, all-knowing, and total love	36
52	If ever, Lord, we meet to praise your name	30
60	Living God, we pray for the Church and for the world	36
62	Lord of all human life	37
53	Lord, we pray 'give us this day our daily bread!'	30
56	Lord Jesus, you set a child in our midst as a potent symbol	33
57	Loving God, your kingdom is a kingdom of justice and mercy	34
54	Loving God, we come to pray for the world	31
59	The storms rage, the waves roll high	35

Commitment

66	Eternal God, you hold in love all who know and praise you	39
67	God of all circumstances and places	39
64	Lord, we have remembered your redeeming love	38
63	Love of the Father, reaching out in creation	38
65	Loving God, you have chosen us	38
68	May the God who is perfectly at home	40
69	Passionate God, our hearts are stirred to life	40

Number	First line	Page

The Lord's Supper

Number	First line	Page
84	As bread is broken for the world	52
85	As you have been fed at this table	53
75	Broken man; Christ crucified; poured-out life	45
76	Can we, who every day eat more than meets our need	46
87	Encircle us with your power	53
80	Father God, you have never left us orphaned	50
88	God of travail, at one with Mary in pregnancy and birth	54
72	God of holiness and love	44
81	Holy God, for the universe you have made	51
90	In the beginning – one God, one world	55
77	Let us give thanks for humble and unassuming mediators	47
86	Like grapes on a sun-drenched hill	53
92	Living God, host and guest, you have been present with us	55
91	Living God, with all your saints, past, present and future	55
70	Living God, host and guest, we await you	43
89	Lord, we have seen your promised victory	54
82	Lord Jesus Christ, you are for us our bread of life	51
78	Lord, we lift our hearts to you	48
71	The fire is lit, the table set	43
79	We thank you, gracious God	49
73	We have heard of one whose life and limbs were broken	44
83	What we have seen and heard, touched and tasted	52
74	Who can sit at this table?	45

Vestry Prayers

Number	First line	Page
104	As the people of God gather for worship	62
105	Father, today you have given us a time to meet together	62
108	Gather us, O God, that we may come expectant to worship	63
100	God, present, available, active, welcoming	61
110	God, Creator, Enfolder, Sustainer, we come to you	64
98	God, you have given us this day	60
96	Grant us peace, Lord	59
99	Let us keep silence as we prepare to worship	60
97	Listening God, may worship happen here today	60
101	Living God, through this worship unite our spirits	61
109	Lord, in our praise and in our prayer	64
103	Lord, as we get ready to go into church	62
107	Lord, now take from our minds all that intrudes	63
94	O God, may this place and this hour	59
102	Spirit of God, uplift those who will lead our worship today	61

Number	First line	Page
106	This day, O God, may our lips sing out in praise	63
93	To you, our God, be all the glory	59
95	What privilege to serve in the sanctuary of praise!	59

The Church Community

A Local and International Community

Number	First line	Page
128	Almighty God, you ever call people	79
126	Bless your Church, loving God!	78
120	Eternal God, with all who have gone before us	73
129	Gracious God, we pray that people will see	80
116	Gracious, patient God, you must have wept	70
114	Heavenly Father, how glad we are to come to church	68
125	Living God, you have set the Church in the world	77
111	Living God, you have promised your presence	67
131	Lord Jesus, where your Church is wealthy	81
117	Lord, you made the world and everything in it	71
115	Loving God, present throughout the world	69
121	Loving God, we give you thanks for our church	74
119	Loving God, you call each of us to ministry	72
118	Merciful God, we rejoice that you entered the world	72
124	O Christ, does a mother stop	76
123	Thank you, living God	75
122	Thanks be to you, Loving God	74
112	We come as a gathered group of your people	67
130	We pray that the Church in every land	81
113	We are your people, loving God	67
127	We rejoice that the Church is no mere huddle of the holy	79

A Reconciled Community

Number	First line	Page
132	From the corners of the world	82
136	God our Healer, in sorrow and shame	83
137	How can we seek the warm safety of worship	84
138	Living, loving Lord of faith	85
141	Lord, as we grow older, help us to remember	86
135	Lord, When we look into the face of someone we know	83
134	Loving Father God, we come as one family to worship you	82
139	O God of all youth, we pray to you	85
140	Our God, you call us to be Church	86
133	Reconciling God, We come as old and young	82
143	We commit ourselves to the tasks of gardening	88
142	We affirm the glory of God's creation	87

Number	First line	Page

Mission and Ministry

Communicating the Gospel

Number	First line	Page
165	Almighty God, who called Abraham to leave his land	103
158	Bless you Church – here and around the world	100
168	Calling God, your voice was known in Creation	104
148	Eternal God, you are a God of good news	93
147	Eternal God, Father and Lord	92
144	Gracious and eternal God, maker, redeemer and inspirer	91
146	Gracious God, calling people to service	91
149	Gracious God, we stand amazed that you call us	93
169	Hands can fight, and push, and shove	104
162	Help us, Father God, to put the gospel into action	101
161	How many people Jesus met!	101
155	If only we could leave it in the past, eternal God	97
160	Living God, bless your Church in the world	100
164	Living God, seen in the face of Christ	103
163	Living God, how beautiful are the feet of those	102
157	Living God, today our thanks are for the transparent saints	99
170	Lord, we need a new spirit and a new confidence	105
145	Loving God, we pray we know your Spirit in us	91
166	Loving God, Jesus your Son lived our life	103
159	Loving God, whose living Word is active now	100
151	Merciful God, accept, we pray, the sorrow we express	95
152	Patient God, we are foolish friends of Jesus	95
153	Seldom-silent God, we thank you	96
156	Thank you, God, for your Word	98
167	We remember, calling God	104
154	We thank you for the Bible and its insights	97
150	We confess our sin, gracious God	94

Learning and Teaching

Number	First line	Page
182	As a shepherd seeks the lost sheep	113
176	Father, we do not find it easy to retain our enthusiasm	108
177	Father, our world is crying out for wise thoughts	109
171	Jesus, through your roots in a Jewish home	106
190	Jesus, teacher, do I hear you clearly?	117
186	Lord God, give us your strength	115
187	Lord Jesus, your teaching was given in the language of the people	116
188	Lord, I know your commandments off by heart	116
175	Lord, a blind and blinkered world cries out for help	108

Number	First line	Page
184	Lord, we keep listening for your voice in the wrong places	114
172	Lord Jesus Christ, we pray that we	106
181	Lord, let silence speak and teach its own truth	112
180	O God, patient and forgiving	112
183	O Creator of the earth, save us	113
178	Precious beyond jewels is the treasure of your Word	110
179	Risen Jesus, where else can we go?	111
173	Risen Christ, as ice melts and rivers flow	107
185	Thank you, Father, for the timeless words	115
174	Too many words spoken without thought fill our lives	107
189	When the prophets of doom proclaim the end of the world	116

Silence and Reflection

Number	First line	Page
193	As the grey wave creeps on to the shore	119
196	Breathe in time with the rhythm of the earth	120
191	God of stillness, hold us in your presence	118
199	Gracious God, light of hope in the darkness of confusion	123
197	I stand. I open myself to God	121
198	Let silence be placed around us like a mantle	122
194	Make time to sit in comfort	119
200	Mysterious God, we seek a safe place	123
202	Sending God, now that we find the listening-place within ourselves	123
195	Sometimes I long to call words of praise to me	120
201	Strengthening God, thank you for filling our empty hands	123
192	When nothing is right, when we are weary and lost	118

Justice, Peace and Reconciliation

Number	First line	Page
204	All-seeing God, We confess to you	124
209	God of nations new and old	129
212	God of justice, encircle the earth	131
211	Holy God, our ears are ringing with the sounds of voices	130
203	Living God, your voice is not silent	124
210	Lord, we know we are infinitely precious to you	129
206	Lord, we thank you For all those whom your Spirit has inspired	126
213	Loving God, we come to you wearied and appalled	132
208	Loving King, There is so much injustice in your world	128
205	Scarred, battered, bleeding is your world	125
207	Spirit of God, like the wind you still move over the waters	126
214	We face each other across a raw divide	132

Number	First line	Page

The Servant Church

Number	First line	Page
216	Come, Lord, and bathe our feet	133
228	I confess it, Lord God	139
224	I am weak – give me strength	138
218	It is so easy, Lord, to pass by on the other side	134
215	Jesus, full of compassion	133
221	Living God, you hold all peoples within your loving care	136
220	Lord, we see you at work in the world	135
227	Lord, when I see only blindness	139
225	May our church exist for others	138
226	Parent God, like a mother hen you gather us	139
219	Thank you, God, your thoughts are wiser than our thoughts	135
217	We look and stare, but what do we see?	133
222	When did we see you in prison, Lord?	137
223	You have loved us, help us to love others	138

The World Around Us

The Created World

Number	First line	Page
237	Creator God, Out of nothing you created everything	147
239	Eternal God, Originator of all that we see and know	148
232	God of the sunshine and the darkness	144
236	In creation you have provided a rich feast	146
238	Let us pray for God's creation	147
229	Lord our God, maker of heaven and earth	143
241	Lord, you have given us a special responsibility	149
235	Loving God, We are sorry that we have marred the beauty	146
233	Mother God, you are a God of beauty	145
242	Not ours, O Lord, but yours	149
231	Spirit of God, at the dawn of creation you blew	144
234	The earth is full of your glory, O God	145
230	The earth is the Lord's!	143
240	You give us a world to enjoy	148

The Seasons

Number	First line	Page
257	All-season God, year-round in love and care	156
255	As we bathe in the light and warmth of the summer's sun	156
250	Creator God, in your hands is the gift of time	153
247	Creator God, with the brightness of daylight	151
259	Dying, rising God	157
251	God of change, You who gave us the seasons	154

Number	First line	Page
258	God of all creation, as springtime dawns	157
248	Gracious God, we are sorry that we have not always lived	152
260	Gracious God, from the rising of the sun to its setting	158
253	Gracious God, we pray for your Church and for the world	155
246	Gracious God, in the bright multi-coloured glory of creation	151
268	Hidden God, cocooned in mystery like an animal hibernating	163
262	Lord, we give you thanks for the long days of summer	160
264	Lord, as autumn leaves fall to the earth to feed the coming spring	160
263	Lord, we give you thanks for the richness of autumn	160
261	Lord, we come in the freshness of a new morning	159
266	Lord God, holy and mighty, we come battered by life	162
267	Lord, often we thank you for springtime's surge of life	162
254	Merciful God, how powerful are the symbols for faith	155
249	Origin of the universe, who created order out of chaos	152
245	Ours is the sunlight	150
269	Small birds, blowing like ash on the wind	164
256	Springtime God, coming alive within us	156
244	The sun rises and sets, but your love, O God, ever rises	150
252	We greet the dawning of the day with wonder	155
243	We listen for your word speaking	150
265	Wise and patient God, we turn to you	161

Conservation and the Care of the Earth

Number	First line	Page
281	A Litany of the four elements	172
277	All-embracing God	169
276	Creator God, we thank you for the beauty and wonder	168
275	For the Babel-towers we build	167
279	God our Creator, whose hands in playful labour	170
270	God of the cosmos, attune our ears to hear you	165
274	Great Spirit, still brooding over the world	167
271	Lord our God, forgive us when we fail you	165
273	O God, the delicate balance of your creation	166
278	Please teach us, Lord, a proper sensitivity	169
272	Rainbow God, as long as earth endures	165
280	When we emerge from our thraldom	171

Work and Leisure

Number	First line	Page
289	And then you rested, working God	178
282	Come, Holy Spirit, come, renewer of life	174
287	Creator God, you made the universe	177
292	Easter with us, bountiful God	180
296	Father, even against the odds	182

Number	First line	Page
288	For sweat on the brow and the sense of a job well done	178
285	God in heaven, ruler of the earth	176
295	Lord Jesus, close to the workers of your own time	181
283	Lord of earth and sky	174
294	Reach down, Lord Jesus Christ, to touch and bless	181
284	We confess, good Lord, how easily we deceive ourselves	175
286	We thank you, Lord, for all that has been done	176
290	Weave a web of your presence around me today	179
291	When factories are closed and workers sacked	179
293	Wrapped in the arms of God's love	180

Human Need

Number	First line	Page
298	Forgive us, Lord, as we live in your world	183
302	God be with you in your reality	185
300	Let us pray to God for all who stand in need	184
301	Lord Jesus, you committed yourself to a world	185
297	Lord Jesus, when you lived on earth	183
303	May your pain give birth to hope	185
299	Thank you, God, for simple acts of kindness	184

Christian Life-style

Home and Family

Number	First line	Page
315	Bonding, loving God, from the many peoples of the world	193
310	Eternal God, For the beauty of creation	191
309	Father, forgive us the foolish mistakes we make	190
316	Father and Lord, when people seem to hate each other	194
312	Father God, we thank you that we are made in your image	192
323	Father and Lord, remembering that the hands of Jesus	197
319	For all who are finding life difficult	195
318	God our Lover, as husbands and wives	194
313	God of every family on earth	192
317	Guiding, supporting God, we have learned many things	194
321	Jesus, we are glad you were born a child of Mary	196
322	Jesus, child of Mary, son of Joseph	197
304	Lord of heaven and earth	189
320	Lord Jesus, who once took children on your knee	195
306	Loving God, we come to worship you	189
307	Loving God, Lord of the Church	190
308	Loving God, your care for us is never-ending	190
305	Parent God, you care for us with over-flowing love	189

Number	First line	Page
314	Praise and thank God for all who give themselves to others	193
311	Spirit hovering over our chaos	191

Fruits of the Spirit

Number	First line	Page
324	Creator God, you are life	198
326	Generous God, you are perfect in goodness	199
325	God of north, south, east and west	198
327	Gracious God, where love is replaced by domination	199
332	Holy Spirit, heavenly dove, once brooding	203
330	Holy Spirit, on our lips speak a word of love	202
328	Holy Spirit, you are depth, silence and wholeness	200
329	Life-giving God, you have not left us as orphans	201
331	Spirit of the living God	203

Forgiveness and Reconciliation

Number	First line	Page
340	Go-between Spirit of God	207
338	God of our relating, thank you	206
335	I am sorry, Lord	204
343	In the struggle against destructive forces	208
336	O God, forgive us when ... we lose sight of the ideals	205
337	Out of my pain I confess my hate-filled days	205
333	Reconciler God: we need your forgiveness for our failures	204
334	Spirit of integrity and peace	204
342	Take our hatreds: make them into handshakes	208
339	The sufferings of the world are yours	206
341	We believe in God: creator and farmer	208

Following Jesus

Number	First line	Page
357	All that I am is yours, Lord	215
355	Christ our advocate, we pray for our sisters and brothers	214
351	Disturbing stranger, you call and we follow	211
347	Forgive us when our lives are guided by desires	210
349	Give thanks to God for those who first introduced you to the way	210
352	God of all life, who wills to us all	212
344	Holy Spirit of God, guide us	209
356	Lord, I may not have the great oratory of the preacher	214
345	Lord Jesus, we follow you because we trust you	209
358	Lord Jesus Christ, you have never spurned or rejected	215
346	Lord Jesus, your 'Follow me' still echoes	209
350	Loving God, we thank you for all those who have listened	211
348	Merciful God, we have promised to be followers	210

Number	First line	Page
354	'One more step along the world we go'	213
353	Our confidence is in you, loving God	212

Personal Service

Number	First line	Page
362	Creator God, For making the world to be our home	218
360	Generous God, you love me 'just as I am'	216
363	God of justice and compassion	218
365	Lord, like Moses bearing the agony of the oppressed	219
364	Lord, you have called us	219
359	Lord, we have heard you call us	216
361	Lord, you have called me to serve you	217

Responding to Suffering

Number	First line	Page
371	As winter trees stretch out bare arms	222
368	For all the times we have acted without love	221
370	For the greening of trees	221
374	God of beauty and power, healing and silence	224
369	Gracious God, even when the swirl of pain seems set to engulf us	221
376	Gracious God, we pray we may become the compassion of Christ	225
378	How is it, Lord?	226
366	In the clash and clamour of life	220
377	Like a thousand springs bubbling up	225
372	Living God, you always seem out of reach	223
373	Loving God, in Christ you are uncompromising compassion	223
375	'Lucky to be alive', we tell ourselves	224
367	We cannot tell how much the sound of silence	220

Offertory Prayers

Number	First line	Page
384	Bless the offering we bring, Lord God	230
380	Lord, we offer you these gifts of money	229
382	Loving Father, All that we have	229
381	Loving God, Our Creator, who gives us life and meaning	229
383	Money, Lord, the love of which is the root of all evil	230
385	Take, Lord, bless and use the offering we bring	230
379	To the God of us all; the God who gives	229
387	What evil, Lord, these notes, these coins	231
386	What folly, Lord, to think that we could bring	231

Closing Prayers and Blessings

Number	First line	Page
392	As you were in the ebb and flow	235
404	As you continue on your way	238

Number	First line	Page
401	Bless to us, O God, the doors we open	238
388	Door of the sheepfold, open to your people	235
396	Go our from here with a pocket full of free gifts	237
397	Go from this place in peace	237
400	God, imbue our souls with calm	238
399	God of beginnings and endings	237
389	God our Shelter in the Storm, protect us!	235
403	May the God of all ages, who is the ever-young	238
398	May the mystery of God beckon us	237
390	O God: Be to us the soil in which we grow	235
402	The love of the faithful Creator	238
394	We have laid our burdens down	236
393	Wherever we go, may the joy of God the Gracious	236
391	You are the Way we shall walk	235
395	You are the Body of Christ	236

Prayers Before Meetings

Business Meetings

406	Father, inspire us, as we discuss the worship and witness	241
408	Holy Spirit, be present with us as we meet together	242
409	Lord God, lead us into your future	242
410	Lord, we are not here to maintain the status quo	242
407	Lord, you were the child of a carpenter	241
405	Lord of the Church	241

Study Groups

411	God, you inspired the writing of Holy Scripture	243
414	Holy Spirit of truth, as we meet to read the Bible	244
412	Jesus, you lived by the Scriptures	243
416	Lord, we make no bones about our ignorance	244
413	Lord, as we meet together, throw light on what we read	243
415	Lord God, make us people of faith!	214

House Groups

420	Father, help us to relax and be ourselves	250
417	God: Father, Son and Holy Spirit	245
418	Jesus, Son of God, you gathered together the disciples	245
419	Let us thank God for this home in which we meet	245
422	Lord, hasten the day	250
421	Lord Jesus, who visited Peter's home and healed his mother-in-law	250
423	Spirit of God, we pray that in our meeting	250

Prayers for Christian Worship
Book 1

Seasons and Celebrations

Compiled by Donald Hilton and written by the same ecumenical team as *The Word in the World.*

The Christian Year

Advent
Christmas
Epiphany
Lent
Transfiguration to Calvary
Mothering Sunday
Easter
Ascension, Pentecost and Trinity
All Saints

The Parallel Christian Year

New Year
Week of Prayer for Christian Unity
Education Sunday
Christian Aid Week
Harvest
One World Week
Justice and Peace
Remembrance Sunday
The Church Anniversary